101 Inclusive & SEN Maths Lessons

of related interest

Practical Mathematics for Children with an Autism Spectrum Disorder and Other Developmental Delays
Jo Adkins and Sue Larkey
ISBN 978 1 84905 400 3
eISBN 978 0 85700 783 4

Common SENse for the Inclusive Classroom
How Teachers Can Maximise Existing Skills
to Support Special Educational Needs
Richard Hanks
ISBN 978 1 84905 057 9
ISBN 978 1 84985 697 3 [Large print]
eISBN 978 0 85700 247 1

Count Me In!
Ideas for Actively Engaging Students in Inclusive Classrooms
Richard Rose and Michael Shevlin
Foreword by Paul Cooper
ISBN 978 1 84310 955 6
eISBN 978 0 85700 377 5
Part of the Innovative Learning for All Series

Making it a Success
Practical Strategies and Worksheets for Teaching
Students with Autism Spectrum Disorder
Sue Larkey
Foreword by Tony Attwood
ISBN 978 1 84310 204 5
eISBN 978 1 84985 683 6

101 Inclusive & SEN Maths Lessons

FUN ACTIVITIES & LESSON PLANS
for P Level Learning

Claire Brewer and Kate Bradley

Jessica Kingsley *Publishers*
London and Philadelphia

Contains public sector information licensed under the Open Government Licence v2.0.

First published in 2017
by Jessica Kingsley Publishers
73 Collier Street
London N1 9BE, UK
and
400 Market Street, Suite 400
Philadelphia, PA 19106, USA

www.jkp.com

Library of Congress Cataloging in Publication Data
Names: Brewer, Claire. | Bradley, Kate (Kathryn D.)
Title: 101 inclusive and SEN maths activities : fun activities and lesson
    plans for P level learning / Claire Brewer and Kate Bradley.
Other titles: One hundred one inclusive and SEN maths activities
Description: London ; Philadelphia : Jessica Kingsley Publishers, 2017.
Identifiers: LCCN 2016027030 | ISBN 9781785921018 (alk. paper)
Subjects: LCSH: Mathematics--Study and teaching (Elementary)--Activity
    programs.
Classification: LCC QA135.6 .B688 2017 | DDC 372.7--dc23 LC record available at https://lccn.loc.
gov/2016027030

British Library Cataloguing in Publication Data
A CIP catalogue record for this book is available from the British Library

ISBN 978 1 78592 101 8
eISBN 978 1 78450 364 2

Printed and bound in Great Britain

Contents

SHAPE, SPACE AND MEASURE

Introduction

Hello,

Thank you for picking up our maths book. As we are both busy, full-time teachers, we understand the demands of teaching fun, creative, appropriate, differentiated, adapted lessons that all the children in your class will love to learn and engage with.

We are both teaching children who are on the cusp of beginning to access the national curriculum learning, and when looking for ideas for lessons to teach the children we found it hard to come up with anything. So the idea for this book was formed.

We believe that when working with children, especially those with special educational needs (SEN), lessons need to meet their interests as well as their needs by containing visual stimuli, movement and fine and gross motor skills, to name but a few! Sitting at a workstation doing worksheets is a sure-fire way to lose a child's attention.

What needs to be remembered is that the children you work with are individuals and so, like any other planning you may do, think about the child and tweak the activity to suit their needs. The lessons included in this book fall under three main categories:

- Using and Applying

- Number

- Shape, Space and Measure.

Within each chapter, the lessons start at P4 and work up towards P8.* Plenaries have been included for each lesson in order to provide an obvious end point for

---

*   All P level descriptors have been taken from the Department for Education. Department for Education (2014) *Performance – P Scale: Attainment targets for pupils with special educational needs.* Statutory Guidance Paper. London: DfE.

the child. We have included ideas for ways to consolidate learning, as doing an activity once with children with SEN is unlikely to support their understanding of a concept.

The book also includes a chapter of starters designed to engage children in motivating learning styles from the beginning of each lesson. It is up to you to decide which starters suit which lesson you are teaching, as you may want to meet a range of additional skills in one session.

We thoroughly enjoyed drawing on our extensive teaching experience to write this book. We hope that it provides you with practical, creative and inspiring lessons that will engage all the learners in your class.

What do we mean by additional skills?

- Kinaesthetic: movement is important to stimulate the child and provide learning experiences that do not revolve around sitting at a table and chair.

- Auditory: being able to develop listening and processing skills in a variety of subjects across the school day will support children to become more attentive in lessons and life.

- Fine motor: these are the skills that involve doing activities on a smaller scale. Developing these skills supports handwriting, dressing and manipulation in the long term.

- Gross motor: these involve the big muscle groups in the body and are large-scale movements. Developing these skills supports trunk control, coordination and motor planning.

- Tactile: skin covers the entire body and is the largest sensory system. Difficulties processing tactile input (such as getting messy) mean that children don't explore and experience the world to its full potential.

- Attention: a child's ability to attain and engage in activities to their full extent needs time and patience. The ability to focus on an individual activity for a longer period of time enables learning to take place. By providing exciting, short activities you can build a child's tolerance to this.

- Oral motor: for children who put things in their mouths beyond expected development it is useful to provide alternate activities that involve the mouth to develop blowing, sucking, chewing and swallowing skills. These movements support the development of speech and successful eating.

- Communication: this is about receptive (listening to) and expressive (responding to) language. Language does not have to be speech; it can be in the form of visuals, switches and gestures.

- Social communication: this is about the vital skills of sharing time and experience with a partner, turn taking and knowing rules within social situations and games.

- Visual: some children rely heavily on their visual system to get cues and stimuli from the world. This can be enhanced through activities that require movement tracking, search and locate and resources that affect the way that light is taken into the eyes (spinning toys, blindfold games, etc.).

- Hand–eye coordination: this skill requires the eyes to interpret a situation and then send messages to the brain, which in turn sends motor messages to the hands to carry out gross and fine motor skills. Practice often improves this skill.

Resources

This is not an exhaustive list, but where possible we have used resources that we find easily in our own classrooms so that life is not made harder for you by having to go out of your way to prepare extra resources for the lessons.

Resources that you will use throughout the book include:

- builder's tray

- choosing board (large, firm board with strips of Velcro to attach symbols and pictures)

- water tray

- balls

- play dough (or a play dough recipe and ingredients)

- shaving foam or play foam

- musical instruments

- small world characters (these are toys that children can be imaginative with – animals, dinosaurs, people, etc.)

- toy cars

- toy trains

- whiteboard and pens

- number fans (a maths resource containing numbers on each arm of the fan)

- chalk

- five ducks, frogs and monkeys

- electronic tablet

- glitter

- sensory toys (flashing balls, massage cream, hand massagers)

- canvas bag

- finish box

- scissors

- teddy bears

- boxes of different sizes

- tubes or ramps.

STARTERS

Dice Game

RESOURCES

Two large dice

Six number cards on each face of one dice

Six action cards on each face of the other dice

ACTIVITY

- The children sit in a circle on the carpet.

- The teacher chooses a child to roll both dice; the child then reads the dice and completes the action; for example, if dice one reads five and dice two reads star jumps, the child completes five star jumps.

Pass the Parcel

RESOURCES

A 'Pass the parcel' set-up with shape symbols in each layer

Range of matching 2D shapes

ACTIVITY

- The children sit in a circle.

- In the middle of the circle an adult places all the 2D shapes so the children can see them clearly.

- Play 'Pass the parcel'. Each time the music stops and a child unwraps a layer to reveal a shape card, the child has to find the matching shape from the middle of the circle.

- At the end of the game, count all the shapes and see who has the most!

Mirror, Mirror

RESOURCES

A mirror

ACTIVITY

- An adult models how an object or person is the same in the mirror.

- Choose two children to stand opposite each other.

- One child makes a movement and the other child copies or 'mirrors' their friend's movement.

- Swap over.

- Allow children to choose two more friends.

Foamy Maths

RESOURCES

Builder's tray

Shaving foam

Paintbrush (optional)

ACTIVITY

- The children sit around the builder's tray.

- An adult sprays the shaving foam into the tray and uses hands or a brush to cover the tray in shaving foam.

- The adult draws a number in the foam and encourages children to say and clap that number.

Teaching note: depending on level of the children, this can be easily adapted; for example, write simple sums in the foam and encourage the children to answer.

Who Has the Same?

RESOURCES

Laminated '1' and '2' number cards or laminated shape cards

ACTIVITY

- The children sit on the carpet.

- An adult hands out the number or shape cards face down to each child.

- Each child looks at their card and then has to find other children in the group with the same number or shape.

Teaching note: this activity can be extended by: using larger numbers; some cards having sums on them and others having the answers so children have to find the child with the answer to their sum; having shape descriptions so that children have to use more language to find their matching partner; using children's faces so that they have to describe faces to each other to find their matching partner.

Magic Number

RESOURCES

Whiteboard and pen for each child or number fan for each child

ACTIVITY

- The teacher tells the children that they are thinking of a number.

- Give the children some clues, such as 'It is one more than three or two times two.'

- Ask the children to write the number on the board or find it on the number fan. After a few minutes say 'One, two, three, show me' and ask the class to show their numbers.

- Everyone puts the board down and claps or stamps the total, and then takes another turn.

Guess from a Line

RESOURCES

Drawing program open on an Interactive Whiteboard

Interactive Whiteboard pen

Bag of pictures of shapes (or pictures made up of shapes as an extension)

ACTIVITY

- The child chooses a shape from the bag.

- On the Interactive Whiteboard, the child draws the first part of the shape. Can anyone guess what the shape is?

- The child draws the next part of the shape, and the group takes more guesses.

Teaching note: change from a single shape to a picture made up of shapes and get the children to guess what the picture is that is being drawn.

You Can Never Guess

RESOURCES

Two large dice

Whiteboard and pen for each child

Calculator

ACTIVITY

- Ask a child to roll the two dice.

- Everyone writes the number sentence on the board. Take the dice away.

- The teacher tells the class that they are going to work out the answer, but that it is too hard and it's unlikely it will be correct! (Make this exaggerated; ask the other staff if they know the answer.)

- Tell the children to put the big number in their head and hold up the fingers of the smaller number.

- Tap the forehead and say the big number out loud and then count on, pointing the raised fingers.

- When the children say the answer, again make a big fuss of how it can't be right – it's too hard. Ask a child to use a calculator and work out the answer.

- When the child shows a correct answer and the children realise they were right, make a big cheer and a lot of fuss. Repeat.

Teaching note: when the children get used to this, change it to two rolls of two dice to create a double-digit addition. Add the units first using the method and then the tens. Check with the calculator.

What's Missing

RESOURCES

Tray

Shiny cloth

Massage cream

Handheld shoulder massager

Wind-up toy

Flashing ball

Laminated pictures of each item

ACTIVITY

- The teacher places all the items on the tray and asks the children to look carefully.

- The teacher tells the children whose turn it is going to be and covers the toys.

- The teacher takes one toy away and lifts the cloth.

- Place the laminated pictures in front of the child and ask them to identify which item has been taken.

- When they make a correct guess, the teacher presents them with the item and they take a turn. Repeat with the group.

Teaching note: to make this more challenging, take away the picture cards or add more items. To make it easier add only two or three items to the tray.

Number Towers

RESOURCES

Construction bricks

Laminated number cards

Bag

ACTIVITY

- Each child and the teacher have a pile of construction bricks in front of them.

- The teacher reaches into the bag and takes out a number. When the teacher says 'Ready, steady, go' all the children need to build a tower with that number of bricks.

- Count the bricks together.

- The next child takes a number out of the bag and says 'Ready, steady, go.' Continue around the group.

Teaching note: to add a further challenge, instead of numbers in the bag, put repeating patterns that the children need to build.

USING AND APPLYING

1. Swap It

Learning Objective

P4 pupils show awareness of cause and effect in familiar mathematical activities.

Additional Skills

Kinaesthetic: handing over a coin to an adult.

Auditory: listening to instructions and ideas.

Fine motor: activating toys.

Tactile: feeling into a bag to find a desired object.

Resources

Laminated coins

Bag with motivators

One-minute timer

MAIN

• The adult gives the child five large laminated coins and counts these out as they are given.

• The adult has a really shiny bag full of motivating toys for the child (spinning tops, bubbles, water spray, car, etc.).

• The child hands over a coin to the adult and they get to choose an item from the bag. A one-minute timer is used and then the item is placed back in the bag. Repeat.

• Control the length of the activity by giving the child more or fewer coins depending on their attention span.

PLENARY

The child is supported to ask a peer if they would like a turn. The peer gives the child a coin and they get a choice from the bag.

CONSOLIDATION ACTIVITY

This activity can be carried out in a small group during quiet time to support the child learning to take turns.

2. Tower Tumble

Learning Objective

P4 pupils show awareness of cause and effect in familiar mathematical activities.

Additional Skills

Gross motor: building a tower.

Kinaesthetic: moving around the room to collect fallen bricks.

Auditory: listening to the song and waiting for the cue to knock the tower down.

Attention: concentrating on the activity for longer periods of time.

Resources

Bricks or construction materials

Small world characters

MAIN

• With a pile of construction materials and a small world figure (wooden bricks, boxes, plastic bricks, etc.) the adult models building the tower: 'One brick, two brick, three brick, more; four brick, five brick, six brick, soar; seven brick, eight brick, nine brick, score; ten brick, stop, put the (man) on top.'

• 'Ready, steady, go!' The child can knock the tower down.

• Repeat, encouraging the child to build the tower and to wait until it gets to ten before knocking it down.

PLENARY

With a small group of children play 'Ten in the bed', starting with however many you have. Ask them to lie down, place a sheet over themselves and sing the song. Each time one should roll out until there is only one left.

CONSOLIDATION ACTIVITY

This game can be played with large construction materials in the outdoor area. If you have a soft play area, the tower could be out of cushions (maybe only five) and a teddy could sit on top and be pushed off.

3. Blow Us Away!

Learning Objective

P4 pupils are aware of cause and effect in familiar mathematical activities.

Additional Skills

Oral motor: forming an 'o' shape with the mouth.

Fine motor: manipulating the straw.

Visual: tracking the movement of the flour/oats.

Resources

Builder's tray

Smaller trays

Oats and/or flour

Straws

A4 or larger laminated numbers

A4 or larger laminated pictures of themselves and classmates

A4 or larger laminated pictures of their favourite activity/toy

MAIN

• Place large laminated photos in the builder's tray and cover them with oats or flour.

• The adult demonstrates using a straw to reveal part of the number underneath.

• The child then uses the straw to blow all the oats/flour out of the way to reveal the whole number.

• The adult and child then clap the number amount.

• Repeat for different numbers.

PLENARY

Place photos of the child and their classmates in smaller trays and cover with oats or flour. Working in a small group all the children blow oats/flour out of the way to reveal photos of the classmates. The children identify the classmate they have revealed.

CONSOLIDATION ACTIVITY

Set up a tray with a picture of the child's favourite toy/activity and cover with oats/flour. Use the straw to blow away oats/flour to reveal the picture. Encourage the child to exchange the picture of their favourite toy/activity.

4. Play Dough Squash!

Learning Objective

P4 pupils show awareness of changes in shape.

Additional Skills

Tactile: experiencing the texture of play dough.

Visual: noticing changes and differences.

Kinaesthetic: movement of squashing the play dough.

Fine motor: rolling the play dough into different shapes.

Resources

Large laminated shapes

Shape symbols

Play dough

Slinky-type plastic springs

MAIN

- The adult models rolling play dough into a ball.
- The child rolls the play dough into a ball.
- The child chooses a shape.
- The child squashes the play dough over the shape until it is completely covered.
- The adult supports the child to choose a symbol to identify the shape they have made.
- Re-roll the play dough into a ball and repeat with another shape.

PLENARY

The adult holds up shape symbols and the child matches them to large laminated shapes.

CONSOLIDATION ACTIVITY

In a small group, inside or outside in the playground, encourage the child with a small group of classmates to play with Slinkys, noticing the way they change shape when moved differently. What shapes can you make with them?

5. Frog Flop!

Learning Objective

P4 pupils show awareness of quantity.

Additional Skills

Visual: tracking movement of frogs.

Kinaesthetic: movement to place frog back on the log or push frog in the pond.

Auditory: recognising familiar song, following verbal cues.

Oral motor: forming different lip and mouth movements for song.

Resources

Water tray

Five frogs

'Log'

Number cards '0'–'5'

Small box

MAIN

- The child sits in a circle in a small group.

- The adult sits at the front of circle with the water tray set up with 'log' over the top and five 'frogs' sat on the log. The number cards are set out in front of tray.

- All join in with singing the 'Five little frogs' song. The adult pushes the frog in the pond at the appropriate point in the song.

- Ask one child to come and take a number away – how many are left?

- Repeat for all the frogs.

- Choose a child to come and find the frogs in the pond and put them back on the log.

- Repeat the activity, but choose a different child each time to push the frog in the pond.

PLENARY

In a small group circle have five frogs. Cover for example three frogs with a small box and see if children can say/use symbols to say how many are left or notice that some frogs have disappeared.

CONSOLIDATION ACTIVITY

Have the water tray set up outside with resources on the table next to the water tray. Encourage the child to come and play with resources and/or set up the activity independently.

6. Five Little Ducks

Learning Objective

P4 pupils show awareness of changes in position.

Additional Skills

Kinaesthetic: touching and counting each of the ducks in the tray.

Auditory: listening to the song and numbers.

Gross motor: placing the ducks in and out of the basket.

Tactile: exploring the water and glitter in the tray.

Resources

Builder's tray

Water

Glitter

'0'–'5' number cards

Five ducks

Pondweeds

Finish box

MAIN

- Set up a builder's tray as a pond with water and weeds. Make or use five plastic ducks.
- Put the number cards showing '0'–'5' in the pond. Add glitter to the water.
- Singing 'Five little ducks', encourage the child to point to each duck that is left and count how many there are.
- The adults should use language such as 'gone!'
- Ask the child 'Where is the duck?'

PLENARY

Count the ducks one by one as they go into the finish box.

CONSOLIDATION ACTIVITY

Outside, set up the water tray with reeds and ducks to sing 'Five little ducks'.

7. Follow My Lead

Learning Objective

P4 pupils anticipate, follow and join in with familiar activities when given a contextual clue.

Additional Skills

Kinaesthetic: moving around the table to collect pieces.

Fine motor: putting the train track together.

Visual: watching the actions of the adult.

Auditory: listening to 'your turn, my turn' verbal cues.

Communication: exchanging a photo for a desired object.

Resources (example for train set-up)

Tray

Four trains

Eight pieces of track

Two people

Level crossing

Trees

MAIN

- The aim is to create a scene that the child would like to engage with.

- The tray is prepared with objects listed in the resources section (or other items that the child really enjoys – just make sure you have double of everything).

- The adult takes the first object and places it in front of himself or herself, naming the action ('Track on table').

- The adult looks at the child and says 'Your turn.'

- Please wait at this point for the child to process the situation; this may take a few minutes.

- If the child takes a turn, great – carry on. If not, hand-over-hand support the child in carrying out the action.

- Repeat.

PLENARY

Once the child has created the scene, engage with the child by playing with the toys. Follow their lead and use minimal language for the last part of the session.

CONSOLIDATION ACTIVITY

During free choice time, make some activity cards that show the process of creating a scene that the child can engage with, such as the train set. The adult should model using the visual supports and then withdraw over time so that the child uses the supports independently.

8. Cake Splat!

Learning Objective

P4 pupils anticipate, follow and join in with familiar activities when given a contextual clue.

Additional Skills

Gross motor: splatting the foam cake.

Kinaesthetic: movement of the arm.

Visual: anticipating the next action.

Auditory: following verbal cues.

Oral motor: forming large lip and mouth movements in response to the activity.

Resources

Shaving foam

Builder's tray or smaller trays

Cake cases

A penny/laminated coin

Food colouring

Pipette

Plenty of cleaning-up paper!

Real cakes/fruit/snacks

MAIN

- The child and adult use shaving foam to fill up cake cases.
- The adult sings 'Five currant buns in a baker's shop, big and round with a cherry on the top.' At this point the child uses a pipette to put a food-colouring 'cherry on the top'.
- The adult sings 'Along came _____ with a penny one day' and the child gives the adult a penny/laminated coin.
- The adult sings 'Aaaaaand splat! Took it away!' The child uses their hand to 'splat' the shaving foam!
- Repeat for the rest of the 'cakes'.
- The adult can slowly invite other children to join in with the lesson to build in turn-taking opportunities.

PLENARY

A small group sits in circle. The adult has some real cakes/fruit/snacks. The children are encouraged to come to the adult to exchange a coin for their preferred snack and say how many cakes, for example, are left.

CONSOLIDATION ACTIVITY

Outside set up the tray with the cake splat resources next to it. Encourage the child to initiate the game independently and remember each stage.

9. Hang Them Out

Learning Objective

P5 pupils sort or match objects or pictures by recognising similarities.

Additional Skills

Kinaesthetic: moving around the room to sort and collect socks.

Visual: using colour or shapes to match the items.

Auditory: listening to instructions and ideas.

Fine motor: using pegs.

Tactile: different textures of socks.

Resources

Washing basket of socks

Washing line

Pegs

MAIN

- With a washing line already in place with one of each of the socks pegged onto it, the child is presented with a washing basket, socks and pegs.

- The adult should support the child to match and peg up the second sock.

- The adult should name the colours or patterns as they are working.

PLENARY

Ask the child to unpeg the socks and fold them together so that the teacher can take them home. Present these to the teacher.

CONSOLIDATION ACTIVITY

Using baby clothes and the water tray, the children can wash the baby clothes and match items by style or colour.

10. Party Time

Learning Objective

P5 pupils make sets that each have the same small number of objects.

Additional Skills

Visual: identifying the same items.

Auditory: listening to instructions and ideas.

Gross motor: moving food to plates.

Tactile: different textures of the food items.

Resources

Play food or real food (multiples of the same item, e.g. raisins, apples)

Two teddies

Two plates

MAIN

- Tell the child that there is going to be a teddies' party and they need to help to get it ready.

- Offer the basket of food to the child and model putting the same amount on each plate, naming the numeral (e.g. two raisins).

- Support the child to create two identical plates and then count how many of each you put out. Work with numbers one to three, as this is the number range children are expected to be familiar with at P5.

PLENARY

If using real food, the adult and the child can eat the teddies' party food. If using pretend food, feed the teddies and make lots of eating noises.

CONSOLIDATION ACTIVITY

Read *Goldilocks and the Three Bears* as an extension activity. Count three of each item as you read through the story together.

11. Wrap It Up

Learning Objective

P5 pupils solve simple problems practically.

Additional Skills

Visual: recognising different-sized boxes and toys.

Auditory: listening to instructions and ideas.

Gross motor: wrapping presents.

Fine motor: using scissors.

Attention: focusing for 15 minutes on an activity.

Resources

Four boxes (that match the size of the toys)

Four toys from small to large

Wrapping paper

Scissors

Tape

MAIN

• Show the child a set of four boxes – all very different in size – and four toys. Ask if they can help to wrap the presents.

• Give the child time to think about what boxes they might choose.

• The small toy will fit in the big box; it isn't until they get to the large toy that there is a problem.

• Once the child has had time to explore the different toys in different boxes, support them to use scissors and tape to wrap the presents.

PLENARY

Play 'Pass the parcel' with the wrapped presents and a small group of friends.

CONSOLIDATION ACTIVITY

In order to keep problem solving, ask the children to help put one letter in each bag ready to go home (one-to-one correspondence). Or they could help put the lids on the correct water bottles (matching colour).

12. Car Wash

Learning Objective

P5 pupils sort or match objects or pictures by recognising similarities.

Additional Skills

Visual: tracking movement of a car into and out of bowl to a colour card.

Kinaesthetic: heavy scrubbing movement to wash the car.

Tactile: sensory experience of the water, scrubbing brush and the car pre- and post-wash.

Attention: maintaining concentration to complete the activity.

Resources

Two or three different coloured toy cars painted with one colour

Washing-up bowl

A4 laminated colour cards to match the colour of the toy cars

Coloured beanbags to match the A4 laminated colour cards

Clear plastic trays

Scrubbing brush

Paint/food colouring

Coloured balls

MAIN

- The adult and child line up painted cars next to the washing-up bowl.
- The adult models choosing a car, washing the paint off, looking at the colour then matching it to the correct A4 laminated colour car.
- The child then repeats the activity, choosing a car, washing it and then matching it to the correct A4 laminated colour card.

PLENARY

In a small group, children sit in a semicircle. The adult at the front of the group lines up the colour cards. Give children a coloured beanbag and encourage them to throw it onto the correct colour card.

CONSOLIDATION ACTIVITY

Play the plenary game in the playground with a group of children. Extend the amount of colour cards and coloured beanbags.

13. Number Rhyme Set-Up

Learning Objective

P5 pupils make sets that have the same small number of objects in each.

Additional Skills

Auditory: listening to verbal cues and instructions.
Kinaesthetic: moving objects from one place to another.
Visual: making choices from visual supports.
Attention: being able to redirect attention to different scenarios and maintain focus.

Resources

A 'log' (laminated picture of a log or safe piece of wood)
A 'pond' (laminated picture of a pond or small water tray)
A 'flying saucer' (laminated picture of a flying saucer or a Frisbee)
Three frogs, ducks and spacemen (laminated pictures of frogs, ducks and spacemen or toy versions)
Number cards '1'–'3' (three copies of each number)
Number rhyme choosing cards
Beanbags

MAIN

- The adult shows the child the log, pond and flying saucer.
- The adult models: 'We need one frog on the log' (put one frog on the log), 'One duck in the pond' (put one duck in the pond) and 'One spaceman in the flying saucer' (put one spaceman in the flying saucer).
- The adult asks the child to choose which song to sing using the choosing cards, then the child and adult act out that song, for example singing 'One little speckled frog'.
- The adult then asks the child to put two frogs/ducks/ spacemen in or on the log/pond/flying saucer and repeat the choosing process.
- Repeat the activity making sets of three.

Teaching note: you may want to start with just one or two number rhyme set-ups depending on the child you are working with. This activity could also be done in small groups to encourage group working and turn taking.

PLENARY

In a small group, children sit in a semicircle. At the front lay out three of the same number cards, for example three cards with the number '2' on them. The children have three beanbags each. The adult chooses three children to come up to the front to make sets of two beanbags on each number card. Repeat for different numbers.

CONSOLIDATION ACTIVITY

Take number cards into the playground. Have a group of children stand in a line. Place, for example, three number '3's on the ground and encourage the children to race to make sets of three children on the number card. Repeat for different numbers up to three.

14. Tempting Trains

Learning Objective

P5 pupils solve simple problems practically.

Additional Skills

Social communication: working as part of a small group to achieve a goal.

Fine motor: building the train track.

Communication: using symbols or speech to request a desired object.

Resources

Train set

Pictures/symbols for tracks, trains and other train set related features stuck onto a laminated board

Small motivating toy

MAIN

- The adult and child sit opposite each other. The adult should have a clear plastic box with a train set in it. The child should have a choosing board with pictures/symbols of the train set items.
- The adult models choosing, for example, a symbol of the train track – taking a piece of the track and beginning to make the train track.
- Encourage the child to exchange a picture/symbol for their desired train track items.
- When the child has completed the train track, has the trains, etc., the adult should playfully remove, for example, a piece of the track or the train and encourage the child to solve the problem of getting it back, i.e. exchanging the picture/symbol for the desired item.

Teaching note: if the child's interest is building blocks, cars, dolls, painting, cooking, etc. adapt the pictures/ symbols to reflect this interest. The important point is that the child is motivated to solve the problem of how to get the item they want through appropriate communication.

PLENARY

The adult shows the child a motivating toy, for example a light-up spinning top. Playfully hide the toy behind your back and encourage the child to think about and indicate which hand the toy is in. Allow the child to play with the toy when they find it.

CONSOLIDATION ACTIVITY

At different motivating times throughout the day, the adult should withhold important items – for example: a fork at lunchtime, a clear plastic bag with snacks, only help to put one shoe on to go outside, etc. – and encourage the child to communicate to request the item they need. Make sure to praise 'trying' and don't withhold for too long, so that the child finds this a fun game and not an upsetting experience.

15. I Can Make a Rainbow

Learning Objective

P6 pupils sort objects and materials according to given criteria.

Additional Skills

Auditory: listening to instructions.

Visual: noticing colours.

Communication: naming colours.

Kinaesthetic: child moving around to place items in different places.

Tactile: touching a variety of objects.

Resources

Basket

Picture of a rainbow

Lots of objects and materials in the following colours: red, orange, yellow, green, blue, purple

MAIN

- Present the rainbow basket and a visual of a rainbow to the child.

- The adult and child should work together to create an object rainbow.

- Language should be kept to colour and the adult should model choosing objects and naming the colour before placing them down.

PLENARY

Using an electronic tablet, take a photo of the rainbow of objects that you have made together and talk about the colours that you can see.

CONSOLIDATION ACTIVITY

Outside, using coats, or jumpers when the weather gets warmer, create a clothes rainbow and encourage other children to join in.

16. Musical Matching

Learning Objective

P6 pupils can sort objects and materials according to given criteria.

Additional Skills

Fine motor: manipulating instruments.

Auditory: listening to rhythm.

Visual: finding the same instrument.

Attention: extending attention to 15 minutes.

Resources

Two triangles

Two drums

Two whistles

Two maracas

Two tambourines

Two castanets

Large box

MAIN

- The adult sits in the floor in a quiet space with the music box.
- The adult chooses an instrument and plays a simple rhythm, then pauses.
- Wait to see if the child chooses the same instrument and joins in. If not, the adult places the instrument in their hand and says 'your turn'.
- When you have played the instruments, group them together.
- Ask the child to choose again and play a tune; the adult copies.

PLENARY

As the instruments get placed back in the box, the adult places them in at the same time as the child and says 'Shake, shake, shake' (maracas), 'Bang, bang, bang' (drum), etc.

CONSOLIDATION ACTIVITY

Try a similar activity using body parts. The adult claps their hands three times and waits for the child. The adult then copies what the child is doing. This could build to include other class members.

17. What Colour?

Learning Objective

P6 pupils sort objects and materials according to given criteria.

Additional Skills

Auditory: listening to instructions.

Visual: noticing colours.

Communication: naming colours.

Kinaesthetic: child moving around to place items in different places.

Tactile: touching a variety of objects.

Attention: sustaining attention for an extended period.

Resources

Large selection of coloured cars

Coloured card matching the colours of the cars

Finish box

Whiteboard and pen

Ramp or tube

MAIN

• The adult needs to set up the box of cars with the coloured squares on the carpet.

• Model (to the child) selecting a car and placing this on the correct colour.

• Work with the child to complete matching all the cars.

• To extend the activity, count the cars on each colour, and the adult with a whiteboard and pen should write the number. Use either hand-over-hand or overwriting to support the child to write the number of cars.

• Push all the cars down the tube/ramp and repeat the sorting.

PLENARY

When the activity has finished, set up a ramp with the finish box at the bottom. Show a colour card and ask the child to post down all the cars of the same colour into the finish box.

CONSOLIDATION ACTIVITY

Repeat this activity with another selection of classroom toys, trains, farm animals, dinosaurs, etc.

18. Copy the Marks

Learning Objective

P6 pupils copy simple patterns.

Additional Skills

Auditory: listening to instructions.

Visual: noticing patterns.

Fine motor: pen grip and mark making.

Attention: sustaining attention for an extended period.

Social communication: waiting for a turn.

Resources

Very large piece of paper

Coloured felt tip pens

Large dice with six different patterns (swirl, dots, lines, zigzag, triangle, circle) on the faces

MAIN

• Place a large piece of paper (as big as you can find) on the floor and have a range of coloured felt tip pens available.

• The adult rolls the large dice and models drawing the pattern.

• Hand the dice to the child.

• Where possible, encourage independent mark making, even if it does not fully represent the pattern. If all marks are the same, support hand-over-hand.

PLENARY

The child is asked to put all the resources away in the correct place. This will support matching across the classroom setting.

CONSOLIDATION ACTIVITY

Once the child is familiar with this activity, invite a few children from the class to join in. This will support the children in taking turns and waiting.

19. Back Together

Learning Objective

P6 pupils copy simple sequences.

Additional Skills

Auditory: listening to instructions.

Visual: noticing key features of a picture.

Fine motor: using scissors to develop cutting skills.

Attention: sustaining attention for an extended period.

Social communication: knowing a role within a situation; supporting an adult to complete a task.

Resources

Three favourite character pictures, each printed on A4 paper

Scissors

Glue

Sugar paper

Pen

MAIN

- Cut the child's favourite character picture into four strips in front of them.

- Can you work together to put it back together? Stick the completed picture to the sugar paper.

- Using the next picture, write the numbers of strips along the bottom of the picture. Go one number higher than the numbers the child is practising (this will probably be between three and five but go higher if appropriate). Write the numbers evenly along the bottom of the picture.

- Cut out the picture again – ensuring there is one number on each strip.

- Ask the child to put the picture back together and stick this to the paper.

- Ask the child to cut the third picture to give to the adult to solve.

- Support them with scissor skills where needed.

- Show that you find the task difficult and ask the child for support.

- Stick the third puzzle to the sugar paper.

- Write the child's name on the work.

PLENARY

Complete a simple puzzle together.

CONSOLIDATION ACTIVITY

This activity could be carried out in literacy instead of numbers – use the child's name to support them putting the picture back together. The picture could be from the class story or topic.

20. Master Builder

Learning Objective

P6 pupils copy simple patterns.

Additional Skills

Visual: noticing key features of a picture.

Fine motor: manipulating building blocks.

Kinaesthetic: pulling building blocks apart.

Attention: sustaining attention for an extended period.

Resources

Four picture cards with simple building-block models

Building blocks to complete the models, plus some extra

Finish box

MAIN

- Ask the child to choose a picture from the selection of four.

- Present them with either the exact pieces (if errorless learning is required) or a few more than needed, to offer a challenge.

- Give the child time to look at the picture and resources before beginning to offer any support.

- If after two to three minutes the child is finding it hard to start the task, the adult should choose another picture and begin taking building blocks to build it.

- If this is not encouraging the child, place the first building block that they need on the table and the second in their hand.

- Try not to use too much language; show the child visually instead.

- Once one model has been completed, place this in the finish box and give the child another picture choice.

PLENARY

Pull apart the building block models (this supports the children's sensory systems) and place all the pieces back into the finish box.

CONSOLIDATION ACTIVITY

Pictures of models of large construction toys for outside could be made so that the child begins to generalise skills away from the classroom. They could also work with a partner to create a model and take a photo, which then could be presented to a different group of children to make.

21. Fruit and Vegetable Sort It!

Learning Objective

P6 pupils sort objects and materials according to given criteria.

Additional Skills

Tactile: feeling and tasting different fruits and vegetables.

Visual: recognising similarities.

Social communication: understanding likes and dislikes of others.

Resources

A range of colourful/long/short fruit and vegetables

Trays or baskets

'Criteria' symbols, for example 'colour', 'long', 'short' and 'round'.

'Like' and 'Don't like' symbols

MAIN

- Explore the fruits and vegetables with the child, commenting on similarities and differences.

- The adult models sorting all the fruit and vegetables into trays/baskets by, for example, colour or length.

- Encourage the child to choose criteria from the symbols, for example colour or 'Is it round or long?' Then suggest they sort the fruits and vegetables into trays according to the chosen criteria.

- Choose different fruits and vegetables to taste and sort into 'Like'/'Don't like' trays!

PLENARY

In a small group allow children to choose different fruits and vegetables. As a group sort them into different trays according to who likes or doesn't like them.

CONSOLIDATION ACTIVITY

In a small group, at snack time ask the children to stand in groups according to their favourite snack. In the playground play sorting games; for example, the children group together according to the colour of their coat, hair, shoes, etc.

22. Play Dough Shape Sorting

Learning Objective

P6 pupils sort objects and materials according to given criteria.

Additional Skills

Tactile: feeling the play dough.

Visual: recognising similarities.

Kinaesthetic: moving and rolling the play dough.

Resources

Play dough, or instructions and ingredients to make play dough

Shape cutters

Laminated shape cards

2D shapes

Feely bag

MAIN

• Make or roll out play dough.

• Select a shape cutter (for example a star), make the shape and match it to the correct shape card.

• Make the same shape and match it to the card. Make different shapes and match them to the shape cards.

Teaching note: you could also use number cutters and match them to numbers.

PLENARY

In a feely bag place several different 2D shapes. Sing 'Feely bag, feely bag, what's inside the feely bag? Put your hand in, feel about, when you're ready pull something out,' to the tune of 'Jingle bells'. Encourage the child to pull shapes out of the bag and sort them into piles on the laminated shape card according to their shape.

CONSOLIDATION ACTIVITY

Collect and feel different everyday objects from around the classroom/school/playground and sort them into groups according to shape.

23. On Repeat

Learning Objective

P6 pupils copy simple patterns or sequences.

Additional Skills

Auditory: listening to and copying a simple rhythm.

Visual: watching others and imitating actions.

Tactile: feeling the texture of different instruments.

Social communication: turn taking and listening to others.

Resources

Range of musical instruments

Choosing board with symbols/pictures of musical instruments

Large 'stop' and 'go' symbols

MAIN

- The children sit in a small group.
- The adult asks them to choose a musical instrument from the choosing board. Allow the children to explore making noises with instruments.
- Use the 'stop' symbol to ask for silence.
- The adult says 'my turn' and models a simple rhythm and then says 'your turn' and the children try to copy.
- Repeat this a couple of times.
- The adult then chooses a child to sit at the front.
- The child makes a rhythm or noise with an instrument and the children copy.
- Take turns around the group to listen to each other and copy the rhythms the other children make.

PLENARY

The adult sits at the front of a small group with a drum. The adult bangs a simple rhythm. Choose a child from the group to come up and repeat the pattern on the drum.

CONSOLIDATION ACTIVITY

In the playground make simple rhythms on different equipment such as the slide (it makes a great reverberating noise!) and encourage the child to copy.

24. Mathematical Movement

Learning Objective

P6 pupils copy simple patterns or sequences.

Additional Skills

Auditory: to follow verbal instructions.

Visual: watching others and imitating actions.

Gross motor: making big and small movements.

Social communication: taking part as a member of a group.

Resources

Symbols of chosen movements

A long strip of card to build up a timetable of movements

MAIN

- In a small group, the adult shows the children a movement symbol, for example a ball, and then models making that movement.

- Encourage the children to copy the movement.

- Show the next symbol and model that movement.

- Put the second symbol next to the first symbol on the timetable and model putting the two movements together.

- The children should copy the sequence of movements.

- Build up movements on the timetable to make a sequence of movements that the children can copy.

Teaching note: you can link the movements to your topic; for example, if you are doing 'Under the sea' you could build up a sequence of crabs, dolphins, waves, etc.

PLENARY

At the end of the session everyone stands in a circle. Encourage one child at a time to stand in the middle of the circle and do a movement, and the others copy.

CONSOLIDATION ACTIVITY

In the playground have an 'exercise class' with different movements such as star jumps and running on the spot, and encourage children to copy and join in with exercise sequence.

Take the symbols from the lesson outside and encourage children to make their own sequence for both the child and the adult to follow.

25. Find the Missing Piece

Learning Objective

P7 pupils identify when an object is different and does not belong to a given familiar category.

Additional Skills

Auditory: listening to instructions.

Visual: matching puzzle pieces.

Tactile: discriminating puzzles and sand.

Attention: sustaining attention for an extended period.

Communication: talking through the activity.

Resources

Puzzle

Sand tray

Spades if the child doesn't like to touch sand

Teaspoons

Cars

MAIN

• In the sand tray, hide a range of puzzle pieces. Also hide some items such as a car or a teaspoon.

• Give the child a piece of the puzzle and say that you dropped the rest in the sand tray and they are hidden, so you need help.

• The child will then sift through the tray and find the pieces.

• The adult should observe what happens when the child finds an alternative item.

• If they start playing with it, remind them that you need help to finish the puzzle and they can play at the end if they would like to.

• Complete the puzzle.

PLENARY

Put the puzzle back in the box and give the child time to play with the items that didn't belong at the end of the session.

CONSOLIDATION ACTIVITY

Hide lots of sets of things in the sand tray such as a tea set, aeroplanes and plastic numbers. Make sure that you hide a few items that obviously don't match the set.

26. In a Twist

Learning Objective

P7 pupils respond appropriately to key vocabulary and questions.

Additional Skills

Auditory: listening to instructions.

Visual: matching body parts and colours.

Gross motor: manipulating body parts.

Attention: sustaining attention for an extended period.

Communication: providing instruction.

Resources

A large sheet with four lines of coloured circles – each line of circles must be the same colour

A board divided into four with 'left hand', 'right hand', 'left foot' and 'right foot' each written in one of the quarters and a spinner in the middle; in each quarter have coloured sticker circles that match the colours on the sheet

MAIN

- Lay the sheet on the floor and set up the board with a spinner.

- Ask the child if he or she would like to go first or if they would prefer that the adult goes first.

- Taking five turns each, spin the spinner and either read out the body piece and colour, or ask the children to respond when the adult tells them.

- Physical modelling and support may be needed.

Teaching note: to make it easier, miss out left and right and just use the hand and foot.

PLENARY

Ask a friend to come and take a turn with the child so the adult can take an observation role.

CONSOLIDATION ACTIVITY

Using chalk on the playground make up a grid, as in the large sheet used above. Call out a colour and ask all the children to run to the colour. Get different children to take turns.

27. Where Should the Hat Go?

Learning Objective

P7 pupils complete a range of classification activities using given criteria.

Additional Skills

Auditory: listening to instructions.

Visual: noticing key features of items.

Fine motor: pen control.

Attention: sustaining attention for an extended period.

Resources

Dressing-up clothes and accessories

Boxes or bags

Sticky labels

Pens

MAIN

• The adult empties the dressing-up box onto the carpet and tells the child that it all needs sorting, as someone came in and messed it up.

• Ask the child how they might sort it (by colours, items or outfits).

• Work together to make piles of the clothes and accessories.

PLENARY

Support the child to write labels for each of the groups that have been created, before putting them in boxes or bags.

CONSOLIDATION ACTIVITY

Find something in the classroom that needs sorting – suggestions include separating pens and pencils, stacking chairs in different colours or sorting the teacher's desk by item.

28. Whose Footprint Is It Anyway?

Learning Objective

P7 pupils complete a range of classification activities using given criteria.

Additional Skills

Visual: recognising similarities and differences.

Social communication: taking turns and working as part of a small group.

Auditory: listening to and following instructions.

Communication: explaining ideas.

Resources

Range of laminated animal foot/paw prints

Matching laminated pictures of the animals to the prints they belong to

Sand tray

MAIN

- In a small group the children and the adult explore the different animal foot/paw prints and comment on them.

- See if children can match them to the correct animal!

- The adults gather the laminated foot/paw prints and suggest a criterion to sort them by, for example number of 'toes', whether they belong to two- or four-legged animals, shape of print or colour of animal.

- Keep gathering the foot/paw prints and suggest a different sorting criterion each time.

- Encourage children to talk to each other during the sorting process. See if they can explain their decisions.

PLENARY

Encourage the children to take turns gathering foot/paw prints and suggest a sorting criterion for their friends to think about.

CONSOLIDATION ACTIVITY

In the sand tray hide the laminated foot/paw prints. Encourage the child to dig in the sand to find the foot/paw prints and to sort them independently into different criteria.

29. Critter Criteria

Learning Objective

P7 pupils complete a range of classification activities using given criteria.

Additional Skills

Visual: recognising similarities and differences.

Social communication: taking turns and working as part of a small group.

Auditory: listening to and following instructions.

Communication: answering questions.

Resources

Zoo/farm/pet/sea/pond animals

Laminated criteria symbols or pictures

MAIN

- The children sit in a small group. The adult produces different animals and encourages the children to comment on them, led by adult questioning, for example: 'How many legs does the chicken have? What colour is the crab?'
- The adult places several of the animals in the middle of the group and asks the children to sort them according to different criteria, for example by the number of legs they have, whether they live on the land/in the sea/ on the farm/in the desert or by colour, shape and size.
- The children can either sort the animals onto the laminated criteria symbols or into groups on the carpet/table.
- Gather the animals back in.
- Place the same or different animals in the middle of the group and ask the children to sort them according to a different criterion.

Teaching note: start with just two types of animals, for example farm and sea animals, and slowly build up to include a large range of animals to widen and vary the sorting criteria.

PLENARY

Encourage the children to take turns gathering the animals in and suggesting a sorting criterion for their friends to think about. As the children get familiar with the activity throw in some 'odd one out' animals that will stimulate conversation. For example, ask the children to sort according to how many legs the animals have and include some snakes or snails.

CONSOLIDATION ACTIVITY

Outside, mix all the animals up and have different habitats set up, for example a water tray, zoo and pet shop, and encourage the children to sort animals according to where they live.

30. Where Should I Live?

Learning Objective

P7 pupils identify when an object is different and does not belong to a given familiar category.

Additional Skills

Visual: noticing which objects shouldn't be where they are.

Fine motor: picking up and moving small world objects.

Tactile: experiencing different sensory scenarios.

Social communication: working in small groups to problem solve.

Resources

Farm/zoo/pet/sea/pond animals

Dinosaurs

Cars

Trains and track

Laminated pictures of the above

Laminated and actual habitats, for example: a sensory farm in a builder's tray and the water tray, dinosaurs in the sand tray, a zoo set up for the zoo animals, the train track and the water tray

MAIN

- The adult sets up two different 'scenarios', for example a sensory farm in a builder's tray and the train track next to it.
- Place the farm animals and the trains in the wrong places, for example the sheep on the train track and the trains in the oats on the farm.
- The adult brings over two or three children to explore the scenarios.
- Model language such as 'Oh no, sheep, where should you be?' and encourage the children to sort the objects into where they should be.
- Reset the scenarios and this time add objects that shouldn't be there at all, for example a dinosaur on the farm or a whale on the train track.
- Encourage pupils to notice 'odd ones out' and to problem solve where they should go.
- As the children become familiar with the activity, set up more scenarios and make the odd ones out less obvious so that children have to work harder to notice the differences.

PLENARY

In a small group, on the carpet lay out two laminated habitats, for example the farm and the zoo. Give the children the laminated pictures of three different objects, for example the farm animals, the zoo animals and the cars. Ask them to sort where the pictures go and see if they can problem solve what to do with the odd ones out!

CONSOLIDATION ACTIVITY

After sessions such as PE, line up all the children's shoes but replace some shoes with, for example, toy cars and boxes, and encourage the children to notice that the object is different and use their communication skills to problem solve, for example tell an adult they have the wrong object and ask where their shoe is.

31. What Can You See?

Learning Objective

P7 pupils respond appropriately to key vocabulary and questions.

Additional Skills

Visual: noticing when objects disappear or reappear.

Fine motor: using the number fan or a tripod grip to write numerals.

Communication: responding appropriately to questions.

Social communication: working as part of a group, taking turns and listening to others.

Resources

Tray

Up to ten objects that are the same

Up to ten different objects

Cloth/blanket

Number fans or whiteboards and pens

MAIN

- The children sit in a small group with the adult at the front.

- The adult has the tray with up to ten objects that are the same, covered with the cloth/blanket in front of them.

- The adult makes a big show of removing the cloth and asking the children 'How many _____ are there?'

- Encourage them to hold up their hands or use number fans or whiteboards and pens to respond to questions.

- The adult replaces cloth, removes some of the objects and reveals them again. Again ask 'How many _____ are there?' and encourage the children to answer as before.

- Repeat this a couple of times.

- Ensuring that there are still only ten objects in the tray, replace some of the 'same objects' with some of the 'different objects'.

- Repeat the covering and revealing process and ask more complex questions such as 'How many pink _____ are there?', 'How many cars did I take away?', 'Are there more or fewer dinosaurs this time?'

PLENARY

Encourage a child to come to the front of the group and do the activity for the rest of the group.

CONSOLIDATION ACTIVITY

Across all the activities in P7, question children using key vocabulary such as 'How many?', 'Can you sort _____?', 'What is different?', 'Which has more?', 'Which container has less?'

32. Christmas Patterns

Learning Objective

P8 pupils talk about, recognise and copy simple repeating patterns.

Additional Skills

Auditory: listening to instructions.

Visual: noticing the pattern or colour.

Fine motor: manipulating paper strands.

Attention: sustaining attention for an extended period.

Resources

Strips of coloured/patterned paper or pre-bought paper chains

Glue

Stapler

MAIN

- During Christmas preparations, work with the child to make repeating-pattern paper chains. Start with a simple repeating pattern and then increase the complexity as necessary.

- The adult will present to the child a paper chain that has been started and talk to them about the coloured chains that they are adding.

- Hand the paper chain to the child. Either offer two choices (one correct and one incorrect) or more if appropriate and the child is able.

- At intervals during the session, ask the child to point to each chain and name the colour (or pattern).

- To extend the learning ask 'What comes next?'

PLENARY

Hang the paper chains up around the classroom and discuss their different lengths.

CONSOLIDATION ACTIVITY

The paper chain activity can be adapted to support addition for the child. Have two different colours of paper cut into strips. Write down a simple sum such as 2 + 1 and use two of one colour and one of another colour; ask 'How many are there all together?'

33. Tally It Up

Learning Objective

P8 pupils use their developing mathematical understanding of counting up to ten to solve simple problems encountered in play, games or other work.

Additional Skills

Auditory: listening to responses.

Visual: noticing the colour.

Fine motor: holding a pen, working towards tripod grip.

Attention: sustaining attention for an extended period.

Resources

Whiteboard and pen

Access to a local road or a video clip of a road

MAIN

- If possible, take the child outside to do a real-life experience tally. If this is not possible, find an internet clip of a road that you can play to the child.

- Explain that you are going to count the different coloured cars and keep a tally.

- A tally is one line allocated to each object. If the child understands this, you can introduce the concept of grouping them in fives; if not, work on tally lines only.

- Before watching the road ask the children to name three colours that they might see. Place the colour names into a table on the whiteboard. The adult should have one so that they can model the activity.

- While watching the road, encourage anticipation, for example 'What will we see next?', and ask questions about the colour that has been seen the most.

- When back at the table, count up the tally lines and write the total.

PLENARY

Do a tally of the children in the class. What is their favourite colour car from the three you have chosen? Again, add these up at the end.

CONSOLIDATION ACTIVITY

Work with the child so that they can do tallies in fives. Encourage them to ask their classmates questions and compile tallies: What is the favourite fruit?, What time do they go to bed?, etc. This will encourage social and listening skills.

34. Guess the Bounce

Learning Objective

P8 pupils make simple estimates.

Additional Skills

Auditory: listening to responses.

Visual: noticing the colour.

Fine motor: holding a pen, working towards tripod grip.

Communication: verbalising guesses.

Attention: sustaining attention for an extended period.

Resources

Electronic tablet

Basket of different balls

Whiteboard and pen

MAIN

- Using an electronic tablet ask the child to film you dropping a ball on the floor and letting it bounce.

- Ask the child to guess how many times the ball bounced and write the number down.

- Watch the clip together and count how many times it bounced – how close was their estimate to the answer?

- Repeat this activity with different balls from different heights.

PLENARY

Working with a classmate, ask the children to guess how many times the ball will bounce. The adult should not be involved other than suggesting that the child works with a classmate. The children need to negotiate who is going to film and who is going to bounce the ball. See if the child can follow the process that they worked through with the adult during the main part of the session.

CONSOLIDATION ACTIVITY

In the playground, gather a group of children and have a race. One child has an electronic tablet and films the race. The children are then asked to guess how many seconds it took to run the race. Write these down in chalk on the playground. Replay the video and see who has the closest estimate.

35. Macaroni Maths

Learning Objective

P8 pupils talk about, recognise and copy simple repeating patterns and sequences.

Additional Skills

Fine motor: threading the pasta tubes onto string.

Visual: recognising repeating patterns.

Tactile: feeling the different textures of the painted pasta.

Social communication: working in pairs.

Resources

Pictures/examples of pre-made necklaces

Coloured pasta tubes mixed up together in a box

String

Colour symbols

Building blocks

Laminated building block patterns

MAIN

• The adult and child look at examples/pictures of necklaces made from coloured pasta tubes and discuss the sequence of colour, for example blue, green, red, blue, green, red.

• Use the colour symbols to make a 'plan' of the sequence; for example, from left to right lay out the symbols – blue, green, red.

• The child then selects the correct-colour pasta tubes to copy the repeating sequence and make his or her own necklace.

• The child uses the colour symbols to make their own colour pattern and then uses the coloured pasta tubes to make their own necklace.

PLENARY

The children should work in pairs. Each child designs a repeating colour sequence using the colour symbols. Each child uses the coloured pasta tubes to make the necklace designed by their partner.

CONSOLIDATION ACTIVITY

In a builder's tray mix up the different-coloured building blocks. Encourage the child to choose a laminated building-block pattern card and copy the pattern.

36. Totalling Tallies

Learning Objective

P8 pupils use their developing mathematical understanding of counting up to ten to solve simple problems encountered in play, games or other work.

Additional Skills

Social communication: taking turns, playing games in small groups.

Kinaesthetic: manipulating small world characters to play football.

Fine motor: using a tripod grip on a pen to make tally marks.

Resources

Table with large piece of paper taped to it

A range of dinosaurs and animals (or other small world characters the child engages with, for example pirates and farm animals)

Whiteboard

Whiteboard marker

Soft, small ball

Building blocks

MAIN

- Set up the 'football pitch' – tape a large piece of paper to a table top (or this can be done on the floor).

- On the paper draw out a football pitch.

- Place the building blocks around the edge of the pitch to prevent the ball from flying off!

- Set up the dinosaurs at one end of the pitch, the animals at the other end of the pitch and the ball in the middle.

- Encourage the child to work with a partner (when they are more familiar with the activity they can set it up together).

- On the whiteboard, model making a tally of the score – explain that the first to ten goals will be the winner.

- Each child chooses a team and makes a tally mark for their team each time they score a goal. Encourage the child to keep a running count of their tally marks.

- The first team to score ten goals and make ten tally marks is the winner!

PLENARY

Encourage the child to choose a criterion with a partner, for example eye colour. Use the whiteboard and pen to make a tally mark for each person in the class with blue eyes, brown eyes, etc.

CONSOLIDATION ACTIVITY

Take a whiteboard and pen into the playground and encourage the child to keep score for games being played, using tally marks.

37. A Hand's Length

Learning Objective

P8 pupils make simple estimates.

Additional Skills

Auditory: listening to questions and instructions.

Visual: visually estimating the length of objects.

Fine motor: placing one object carefully in front of another.

Communication: answering questions.

Resources

Ten cut-out handprints previously made by the child

Number cards '1'–'10', whiteboard and pen or number fans

MAIN

- Show the child an object, for example a table, and ask 'How many handprints long is the table?'
- Encourage the child to guess the length through speech, writing the number or showing a number card or number fan.
- Then encourage the child to lay out handprints on the object and see if their estimate was correct!
- Repeat for different objects.
- The activity can be replicated using footprints.

Teaching note: at P8 children are working on numbers up to ten so it is best to keep the length of objects to a maximum length of ten handprints. However, if the child can understand quantity beyond ten, challenge them with longer objects.

PLENARY

The children sit in a small group. The adult chooses a child to come to the front and lie down. Others in the group guess how many handprints tall the child is. Lay out the handprints and see whose estimate was the closest.

CONSOLIDATION ACTIVITY

Around the school and in the playground encourage the child to guess the length of, for example, the slide. Model putting one hand in front of the other and counting to measure the hand lengths of the slide, and see if the estimate was correct.

NUMBER

38. Bang!

Learning Objective

P4 pupils show an awareness of number activities and counting.

Additional Skills

Auditory: using loud noises as a cue for participation.

Tactile: feeling different textures.

Attention: sustaining concentration for short periods of time.

Social communication: waiting for a turn.

Resources

Builder's tray

Shaving foam/large bubble wrap/five drums

Choosing board for the above items

MAIN

- The child sits in front of the adult.

- The adult sets up the builder's tray with five shaving foam blobs/five large pieces of bubble wrap/five drums. The adult counts as they place each object in the tray.

- The adult chants 'Five fat sausages sizzling in a pan.' At this point shake the builder's tray as if it were a frying pan.

- The adult chants 'One went pop and the other went bang!' Shout the word bang and splat/hit the shaving foam/bubble wrap/drums in the tray.

- Encourage the child to clap to make a corresponding noise.

- Repeat for the other four objects left in the tray.

Teaching note: really build up the anticipation before the 'bang' to encourage attention building. When the child is familiar with the activity, encourage them to take part.

PLENARY

In a small group encourage children to choose from the photos their preferred sensory medium to create a 'bang'. Take turns to make the 'bang' in the activity.

CONSOLIDATION ACTIVITY

In the playground chant 'Five fat sausages' with the child, build up the anticipation before the bang and see if they clap at the right time. Make loud bangs on the playground equipment.

39. Spray Me!

Learning Objective

P4 pupils show an awareness of number activities and counting.

Additional Skills

Visual: choosing between two photos/symbols.

Tactile: experiencing different messy media.

Social communication: waiting for a turn.

Oral motor: making an 'o' shape with the mouth.

Resources

Water spray/bubbles/shaving foam

Laminated photos or symbols of messy media

Laminated number symbol cards '1' and '2' (cards should have the numeral then the corresponding amount in dots)

Laminated card to attach the number symbols to

MAIN

• The children sit in a small group.

• Start with, for example, the water spray.

• Ask the child 'One or two?' and encourage them to choose a number symbol and give it to the adult.

• The adult then sprays the child once or twice depending on their choice!

• Let each child take a turn.

• Repeat with the other sensory media (with the bubbles, blow once or twice).

Teaching note: as the child becomes familiar with the activity encourage them to first choose messy media from the photos/symbols and then choose the number symbol.

PLENARY

Encourage and support the child to play the role of the adult, responding to the choices of peers.

CONSOLIDATION ACTIVITY

In small groups in the playground encourage the child to choose an action, for example star jump, and then choose how many times to do the action.

40. Choose a Song

Learning Objective

P4 pupils show an awareness of number activities and counting.

Additional Skills

Auditory: listening to the songs.

Fine motor: exchanging a picture or object.

Tactile: exploring objects.

Social: turn taking.

Communication: making an exchange for an item.

Resources

Laminated pictures of number songs ('Five little ducks', 'Five speckled frogs', 'Five little men in a flying saucer', 'Five little monkeys', etc.) or favourite songs of the child

Canvas bag

One duck, one frog, one alien, one monkey (inside the bag)

MAIN

- Have the choosing bag ready and all the picture cards attached to a board.
- If the child can exchange a picture, offer them the board. If they are at object level, offer them the bag.
- Once they have made a choice, supplement this with the accompanying picture or object.
- Sing the song together and place the items back.
- Choose again.

PLENARY

Sing 'Put all the toys back in the bag, back in the bag, back in the bag, put all the toys back in the bag, for another day,' while supporting the child to tidy up.

CONSOLIDATION ACTIVITY

At points where the child has a free choice, you can offer the singing/choosing bag or the story sack to repeat the activities to increase familiarity.

41. Flying Saucers

Learning Objective

P5 pupils respond to and join in with familiar number rhymes, stories, songs and games.

Additional Skills

Auditory: listen to oral cues.

Communication: respond to cues.

Gross motor: large movements as part of songs.

Kinaesthetic: completing song actions.

Social communication: working in a small group.

Resources

Therapy/large ball or blue material shaped into circle

Pre-made spaceman/ alien masks or hats (not essential!)

MAIN

- In a group of five the children stand around the ball/ material.

- The adult sings 'Five little men in a flying saucer' with actions as follows:

  » 'Flew around the world one day' – children pretend to fly around the ball/material

  » 'They looked left and right' – turn heads left and right

  » 'But they didn't like the sight' – tap foot, shake head and wag finger

  » 'So one man flew away' – one child pretends to fly away from group and sits on the floor until the song has finished.

PLENARY

Everyone lies back on the floor and relaxes. Put one hand in the air showing five fingers; sing the song quietly, this time indicating numbers using fingers.

CONSOLIDATION ACTIVITY

Outside and in the playground play other number rhyme songs such as 'Five little frogs' in a similar way.

42. Roll Me One or Two

Learning Objective

P5 pupils can indicate one or two.

Additional Skills

Tactile: feeling the texture of the play dough.

Visual: recognising if object needs one or two, for example wheels.

Fine motor: rolling the play dough into different shapes.

Communication: commenting on number.

Resources

Play dough or ingredients to make play dough

Laminated play dough mats with pictures of objects that need one or two of something, for example a bike and a unicycle (wheels), a boy and a flamingo (legs), a runner and person in a sack race (shoes), a monster with one eye and a face with two eyes (eyes).

Laminated '1' and '2' number symbols

MAIN

- The adult and child look at the first set of pictures.
- The adult encourages the child to comment.
- The adult models rolling, for example one play dough wheel for the unicycle and two for the bike!
- Repeat for the other pictures, always emphasising counting one and two along with the respective quantity.

PLENARY

Give the child the '1' and '2' number symbols. Look at the pictures again and see if the child can identify which picture has one of the criteria and which has two.

CONSOLIDATION ACTIVITY

Take the number symbols outside. Make a game of seeing if the child can show, for example, one arm waving, two arms waving, hopping on one leg and jumping on two legs.

43. Teddy's Hungry

Learning Objective

P5 pupils demonstrate that they are aware of contrasting quantities.

Additional Skills

Visual: recognising different quantities.

Social communication: beginning to understand how someone else might feel.

Fine motor: sorting objects onto plates.

Attention: maintaining attention as part of a small group.

Resources

Two teddies

Two plates

A selection of play or real food

Laminated '1' and 'lots' symbols

Water spray

MAIN

- Set up the two teddies with the plates in front of them.
- Explain to the child that one teddy wants only one of something and the other wants lots!
- Support the child to sort play/real food onto plates for the teddies.
- Repeat for other types of food.

PLENARY

Show the child the water spray; ask them to choose from the symbols if they would like one or lots of sprays. Respond to their choice.

CONSOLIDATION ACTIVITY

At lunch or snack times offer child a choice of one or lots of, for example, chips, breadsticks or orange segments.

44. Tune Choosing

Learning Objective

P5 pupils respond to and join in with familiar number rhymes, stories, songs and games.

Additional Skills

Auditory: listening to the songs.

Visual: selecting a desired picture.

Communication: making an exchange.

Social communication: sharing an experience with an adult or peer.

Resources

Electronic tablet

Choosing board with pictures of five favourite number rhymes

MAIN

- On an electronic tablet, have five number rhymes prepared in the browser.

- Show the child the choosing board and wait for them to make a request.

- Once the exchange has happened, offer them the tablet and sing the song together.

- Repeat.

PLENARY

On an art program on the tablet, create a picture of one of the number rhymes. How many characters are needed and what happens to them? This may just be mark making, but it provides meaning to the marks.

CONSOLIDATION ACTIVITY

Extend the range of songs and stories that the child has to access on the choosing board. This can be used as a motivating activity after a task that the child may not be as keen to participate in.

45. Two Eyes and One Nose

Learning Objective

P5 pupils can indicate one or two.

Additional Skills

Social communication: taking turns.

Visual: looking in a mirror and finding body parts.

Kinaesthetic: actions to the songs.

Communication: responding to questions.

Resources

One large mirror or a range of small mirrors

Cards with body parts (eyes, nose, arms)

MAIN

- With the mirror set up in front of the adult and child, talk about the different body parts.

- The adult asks questions such as 'How many eyes do you have?' and then they count them together.

- Show a range of body part picture cards, support the child to choose one and then count how many body parts you have together.

PLENARY

Sing 'Head, shoulders, knees and toes'.

CONSOLIDATION ACTIVITY

Once the child is becoming familiar with counting one and two, add finger and toes cards to the selection. Can the child begin counting beyond two with support?

46. More or Less Sensory Bottles

Learning Objective

P5 pupils can demonstrate that they are aware of contrasting quantities.

Additional Skills

Attention: working on a shared project for more than five minutes.

Visual: exploring the sensory bottles.

Social communication: spending time sharing an activity with an adult.

Resources

Plastic bottles of the same size

Jug of water

Classroom resources, for example glitter, sequins, small world, paint, string

MAIN

• Create a selection of sensory bottles with the child.

• Spend time moving around the class and collect resources together that you can use for them.

• Hand-over-hand with the child, support putting a small amount in one bottle and a large amount in the second bottle (of the same item).

• In a darker, quiet space, with torches, spend time with the child exploring the bottles.

• Make comments as they pick up different ones that have more or less.

• Ask the child if they can find the bottle with more.

PLENARY

Spend time together washing up the bottles, or, if you have space to keep them, find a special place where you can find them again another day.

CONSOLIDATION ACTIVITIES

To continue working on the concept of contrasting quantities, in the playground create a gardening area with different-size plant pots, soil and trowels. Say 'more' or 'less' as the child fills the different-size pots with soil and pours it out.

47. Five Car Tunnel Race

Learning Objective

P6 pupils join in by rote counting up to five.

Additional Skills

Visual: noticing the cars.

Fine motor: manipulating cars into the tunnel.

Kinaesthetic: moving to collect the cars.

Communication: responding to instruction.

Resources

Long cardboard tube

Five cars

'1'–'5' laminated number cards

Finish box

MAIN

- Set up the tube against a table with a long space at the bottom.
- Pass the five cars to the child and encourage them to post them down the tube.
- Watch them whizz out of the other end. As they come out, the adult counts them: 'One, two, three, four, five.'
- It is hoped the child will join the rote counting after a while.
- Repeat.

PLENARY

Place a box at the bottom of the tube and, as the cars go down, count them into the finish box: 'One, two, three, four, five, finished.'

CONSOLIDATION ACTIVITY

This activity can be done with trains or different-coloured balls either in the classroom or set up out on the playground down the slide. Ask other children to join in so that they can collect the items as they whizz down.

48. Find Three

Learning Objective

P6 pupils count reliably to three, make sets of up to three objects and use numbers up to three in familiar activities and games.

Additional Skills

Visual: searching and locating.

Attention: engaging for around 10–15 minutes.

Kinaesthetic: moving around the room to find the animals.

Resources

Three of each colour maths sorting animals (bears, dinosaurs, etc.)

A range of coloured cards that match the colours of the animals

MAIN

- Using a set of coloured counting animals, hide these around the classroom or outdoor area. Keep one colour behind and show the child three.

- Use your finger to count each one reliably.

- Support the child to do the same.

- Ask them 'Where are the animals?' Go on a hunt and find as many as you can.

- Back at the table, place the coloured cards down and support the child to sort according to colour.

- Once sorted, count each set. Have all three been found?

- If the child is still engaged at this point and if some are missing, go on another hunt.

PLENARY

Count all the animals colour by colour back into the jar.

CONSOLIDATION ACTIVITY

Ask the child to hide the animals and then approach a favourite peer. Ask if they would like to find the missing animals. Repeat the sorting and counting activity as above.

49. Foam and Seek

Learning Objective

P6 pupils demonstrate an understanding of the concept of more.

Additional Skills

Tactile: tolerate texture and mess.

Visual: seek the favourite image.

Communication: sign or say 'more'.

Fine motor squirting shaving foam.

Resources

Builder's tray

Shaving or play foam

Laminated favourite character

Paintbrush

MAIN

- Set up a builder's tray where being messy won't affect others who are not involved in the activity.
- Place a laminated picture down on the tray. Tell the child that it needs to be hidden.
- Show them a can of foam and squirt some onto the picture.
- Ask the child 'Is the picture covered? No – what do we need? More!'
- Encourage them to sign or say the word. The adult should do another squirt and repeat the question.
- After a few more turns, let the child have the foam.
- Once the picture is covered, either with hands or a brush, try and find the picture again.

PLENARY

While the child is making marks in the foam, the adult can model writing letters and numbers in the foam. Their name and age are often motivating. Can the child copy this?

CONSOLIDATION ACTIVITY

A similar activity can be done by pouring on a little flour at a time or pouring coloured water into a water tray.

50. Teddy Needs Two Clean Socks

Learning Objective

P6 pupils demonstrate an understanding of one-to-one correspondence in a range of contexts.

Additional Skills

Fine motor: making a pincer grip to use a peg.

Visual: matching the colours.

Attention: focusing for more than ten minutes.

Resources

Pairs of different-coloured socks (keep one pair to the side)

Teddy

Water tray

Water

Washing-up liquid

Towel

Washing line

Pegs

MAIN

- Hang up the washing line with the child.
- Ask the child to help you to wash Teddy's socks.
- Only produce one of each colour sock.
- Once you have explored the water tray, work together to hang them on the line.
- The adult should find the other set of socks under the table. Silly Teddy had hidden them!
- Wash these too.
- When it comes to hanging them on the line, support the child to match one sock with the other sock to pair them.

PLENARY

Show the last pair of dry clean socks to the child and ask them to help put them on Teddy.

CONSOLIDATION ACTIVITY

When the socks have dried, put them into pairs. Name the colours and count the socks as you go.

51. Racing Cars

Learning Objective

P6 pupils demonstrate an understanding of one-to-one correspondence in a range of contexts. Pupils join in by rote with counting up to five.

Additional Skills

Visual: recognising that one item goes to each child.

Social communication: working as part of a small group.

Gross motor: pushing the car.

Attention: tracking an object as it moves down the tube.

Resources

Long cardboard or preferably transparent tubes – one for each child

Toy cars

A range of other small world items

Large tray or box with water

Finish box

MAIN

- In a small group, children line up behind the builder's tray or box.

- Encourage the child to give out the tubes, giving one to each classmate using minimal language, for example 'Give tube to _____.'

- Encourage the child to give out the cars, giving one to each classmate, again using clear, minimal language, for example 'Give car to _____.'

- The child takes one tube and one car and joins the group.

- Everyone counts to five and pushes their cars down the tube to splash into the water!

- Repeat the activity, encouraging the child to give out the resources again – one to each child in the group.

Teaching note: as the child becomes familiar with the activity, add other objects such as small world items into the activity so that they have to practise one-to-one correspondence further. The activity can be extended by adding another key word instruction, for example 'Give the red car to _____.'

PLENARY

Encourage the child to give each classmate a paper towel and then retrieve wet objects from the tray or box and give one back to each child to dry. Collect dry objects from each child and place them back in the finish box one at a time.

CONSOLIDATION ACTIVITY

At the end of the day encourage the child to give bags and coats to classmates to extend their understanding of one-to-one correspondence.

52. Farming in Threes

Learning Objective

P6 pupils count reliably to three, make sets of up to three objects and use numbers to three in familiar activities and games.

Additional Skills

Tactile: feeling different textures.

Visual: recognising groups of three.

Auditory: listening to spoken instructions.

Attention: maintaining concentration until a task is complete.

Resources

Dry, messy media, such as oats, flour, cereal

Builder's tray

Building blocks

Farm animals – three of each, for example three pigs, three sheep

Action symbols, for example 'jump', 'hop', 'clap'

MAIN

- Set up the empty builder's tray on one table with all the resources next to the tray.
- Ask the child to help you set up the farm.
- Using three block at a time, ask the child to build 'walls' to make three different areas in the builders tray. Count up to three with the child each time you build part of the wall.
- Ask the child to fill the areas with three handfuls of different messy media.
- Ask the child to make groups of three animals in each area.
- Encourage the child to play with the sensory farm once it is set up.

Teaching note: ensure that you reinforce counting to three each time the child makes a set of three.

PLENARY

Ask the child to tidy up by counting up to three, for example 'Can you put three pigs back in the box?', 'Can you put three builder's blocks back in the box?'

CONSOLIDATION ACTIVITY

In the playground and outside encourage the child to choose an action symbol and complete it three times. Make sure the child counts to three each time and stops! This can be done in larger groups.

53. In the Garden

Learning Objective

P6 pupils demonstrate an understanding of 'more' and join in with new number rhymes, games and songs.

Additional Skills

Tactile: experiencing different messy media.

Social communication: waiting for a turn.

Communication: indicating wanting more of something.

Attention: joining in with a new game and learning a new song and rules.

Resources

Stiff piece of card

Water spray

Shaving foam or play foam

Shower curtain or builder's tray

Chair

Laminated 'more' and 'finish' symbols on a choosing board

MAIN

- The children sit in a semicircle in a small group.

- Set up the chair on the shower curtain or in the builder's tray.

- Choose a child to come and sit in the chair and chant the following rhyme with actions: '_____ is in the garden, blow wind, blow!' Fan the child with the card once. Stop and wait for them to indicate if they want more or to finish, using speech, gesture or by choosing from the symbols.

- Say 'Splish, splash, rain drops!' and spray the child once with the water spray and, as above, wait for them to indicate whether they want more or are finished.

- Say 'And down comes the snow!' and spray a small bit of foam in your palm and clap it over the child's head. Again, wait for them to indicate whether they want more or are finished.

- Encourage the child to choose a friend to be next.

PLENARY

The children sit in a semicircle in a small group; encourage them to choose from the card, water spray or foam. Let them have a small amount of the chosen messy media and encourage them to indicate if they want more.

CONSOLIDATION ACTIVITY

At snack or lunchtimes give the child just a small amount of food and encourage them to indicate that they need more!

54. Place the Pompom

Learning Objective

P7 pupils recognise numerals from one to five and understand that each represents a constant number or amount.

Additional Skills

Visual: recognising quantity to match to numerals.

Attention: focusing on an activity for longer periods of time.

Fine motor: using a pincer grip to pick up different objects.

Resources

Pegs or larger plastic tweezers

Coloured pompoms

Laminated numerals '1'–'5'

Shells and/or pebbles

MAIN

- On a table or on the carpet lay out numerals '1'–'5' and count with the child as you do so.

- Model using the peg/tweezers to place, for example, one pompom on the numeral '1'.

- Encourage the child to complete the remainder of the activity, counting each number out as they do so.

- When the child is familiar with the activity, extend it by having a range of coloured pompoms and ask, for example, 'Can you put three red pompoms on the number "3"?'

PLENARY

Ask the child to tidy up the activity by counting the mpoms back into the box. The adult can extend the activity by asking the child to put, for example, three pompoms back in the box and then add one more.

CONSOLIDATION ACTIVITY

In the sand tray outside have a range of shells and/or pebbles and the number cards. Ask the child to find, for example, five shells and put five shells on the number card.

55. One to Ten – Go!

Learning Objective

P7 pupils join in by rote with counting to ten.

Additional Skills

Fine motor: folding the paper to make the paper aeroplane.

Attention: anticipating the event.

Visual: tracking the aeroplane as it flies.

Communication: using new vocabulary to describe what happened.

Resources

A4 paper

Paper aeroplane instructions

Symbols to help prompt conversation about what happened, for example 'far', 'fell', 'flew', 'landed'

Action symbols

MAIN

- The adult and child follow the instructions to make the paper aeroplane.

- Find a suitable place to throw the plane; in the classroom the adult could make a masking-tape line to see if the planes can reach the line.

- The adult and child count by rote to ten before throwing the plane.

- Talk about what happened – did the plane fly far? Did it cross the line?

- Repeat the activity, always counting by rote to ten first.

PLENARY

This activity could be done in a small group. The adult encourages the child to choose an action from the action symbols and then counts by rote to ten, each time completing the action.

CONSOLIDATION ACTIVITY

Outside on different playground equipment, encourage the child to join in with counting by rote to ten; for example, the child sits on top of the slide and the adult and child count to ten before the adult pushes the child down the slide! Count being pushed on the swing ten times.

56. Who Wants More?

Learning Objective

P7 pupils demonstrate an understanding of 'less'. In practical situations pupils respond to 'add one' to a number of objects.

Additional Skills

Visual: recognising different quantities on a plate.

Communication: responding to requests.

Fine motor: picking up small objects to add one.

Social communication: group work.

Resources

Two teddies

Two plates

A range of real or pretend food

Laminated 'less' symbols

Water bottles filled with different quantities of, for example, glitter water, coloured water.

MAIN

- Set up the teddies at the table or at a picnic with the two plates in front of them.

- The adult places, for example, three cakes on one plate and just one on another plate.

- The adult asks the child 'Which teddy has less cakes?' and the child uses gestures, symbols or speech to indicate the plate with fewer cakes.

- The adult asks the child to add 'one more cake to the plate with less cakes' and then repeat the questioning.

- Repeat this activity for different food items.

Teaching note: once the child is familiar with the questions and the concepts of 'less' and 'adding one' invite some friends to come and play instead of using the teddies.

PLENARY

Ask the children to sit in a small group in a semicircle. The adult produces two water bottles from behind their back and asks the children to indicate which has less using gestures, symbols or speech. Repeat for different bottles.

CONSOLIDATION ACTIVITY

During lessons such as art, ask the child to hand out the crayons; give them different quantities to give to their friends. Ask the child who has fewest crayons and then ask them to add one more to that friend's pile. This could be repeated for snacks.

57. Treasure Hunt

Learning Objective

P7 pupils can count at least five objects reliably.

Additional Skills

Communication: respond to mathematical questions such as 'How many?'

Gross motor: digging in the sand for objects.

Visual: recognising the object and matching it to the photo.

Attention: maintaining concentration and focus for at least 15 minutes as the lesson is extended.

Resources

Range of motivating objects – five of each, for example five laminated gold coins, five cars, five shells

Laminated photos of objects

Sand tray

Small spade

MAIN

- The adult sets up the sand tray so that there are five objects that the children find motivating buried in the sand.

- Show the child the laminated photo of the hidden object and ask them to hunt for them all in the sand!

- When they have all been found and placed on the photo, the child counts them.

- Once the child is familiar with the activity, extend the range of buried items so that the child is reliably counting five different objects once they have all been found and matched to their photos.

PLENARY

The adult asks the child to bury the objects in the sand for another game or another child to play, counting the objects as they bury them in the sand.

CONSOLIDATION ACTIVITY

At different times throughout the day ask the child to give five objects to a friend, for example five crayons or five raisins, counting as they do so.

58. Hungry Faces

Learning Objective

P7 pupils recognise numerals one to five and understand that each represents a constant number or amount.

Additional Skills

Fine motor: using tweezers.

Visual: noticing numerals.

Communication: verbalising numeral names.

Resources

Builder's tray

Pasta (coloured the night before with food colouring)

Tweezers

Six cartoon faces on laminated A4 paper, with a large hole for the mouth (make sure they can stand up)

Counting bowls

Laminated '0'–'5' number cards

Switch or electronic tablet (optional)

Finish box

MAIN

- Set up the builder's tray with the coloured pasta in the centre and tweezers.

- Set up the laminated cartoon faces with large holes for mouths that the child can 'post' the pasta into.

- Put a bowl behind each vertical face and a number next to each one.

- Tell the child that the people are hungry, but they only like to eat a certain number.

- If possible, have a switch or an electronic tablet with sound effects that can be made each time they feed someone.

- Count aloud how many they are feeding each person.

- Check each time, and support them if corrections are needed.

PLENARY

Put the faces in the finish box and count down from the number to zero each time.

CONSOLIDATION ACTIVITY

In a workstation a small version could be set up of this activity, with numbers, coloured bowls and tweezers, with a different selection of things to be picked up each time (pebbles, pompoms, rice, etc.).

59. The 12.22 Midland Train to London

Learning Objective

P7 pupils can count at least five objects reliably.

Additional Skills

Attention: focusing for longer than 15 minutes.

Visual: noticing the numbers.

Gross motor: moving the trains around the track.

Resources

Five train engines

15 train carriages

Large white paper

Marker pens

Stickers

MAIN

- Before the lesson, prepare the train engines by putting stickers with numbers '1'–'5' on them. Put these out of sight.

- Set up a large piece of paper on the floor with some marker pens.

- Tell the child you have lost the train track, so they need to draw one.

- Spend time together drawing straight vertical and horizontal lines to make the track.

- Pass the engines and the set of carriages to the child. Tell them that they need the correct amount of carriages to be able to work.

- Allow the child to try this.

- If they don't understand, model putting three carriages to the number three engine.

- Once the trains are connected, play together on the train tracks; maybe there is a crash and the trains need putting together again!

PLENARY

The adult says 'Number one engine back to the station', and the child leads it into the box. Repeat this with all the trains.

CONSOLIDATION ACTIVITY

A similar activity could be carried out with racing cars with numbers, by putting them into the correct garages. Using a large, white piece of paper, draw a road and five garages. Number the garages and make sure the right car goes to the right place.

60. Up and Away

Learning Objective

P7 pupils join in by rote with counting up to ten.

Additional Skills

Auditory: listening and responding to one's name.

Social communication: working as a whole class group.

Attention: engaging in a group activity for over 15 minutes.

Kinaesthetic: moving the parachute.

Resources

Parachute

MAIN

- *Parachute game one*: get the class group to stand around the edge of the parachute and lift the parachute up and down while counting to ten. When you get to ten, shout out two names and these children run under the parachute and swap places. Repeat.

- *Parachute game two*: get the class group to sit around the edge of the parachute with their feet and legs underneath; one person goes around the group touching the legs while counting from one to ten. Number ten gets pulled under the parachute and they take a turn. Repeat.

PLENARY

Put on some relaxing music and ask all the children to lie under the parachute while the adults waft it up and down. At the end of the session count down from ten to zero and let the parachute fall on top of the class. Pack the parachute away.

CONSOLIDATION ACTIVITY

The parachute can be taken out to the playground and children from other classes could join in with the games.

61. Add One More Duck

Learning Objective

P7 pupils respond by adding one to a number of objects.

Additional Skills

Gross motor: manipulating dice and ducks.

Communication: following instructions.

Auditory: listening and joining in with a song.

Resources

A dice showing the numbers '0'–'4' (use a blank dice and write the numbers on)

Five rubber ducks

Water tray

Water

Finish box

MAIN

- Set the water tray up to look like a pond using any available resources.

- The child is asked to roll the dice. Ask 'How many?' and the child places the number of ducks shown on the dice into the water tray. Then the adult prompts them to add one more duck and asks 'How many altogether?'

- Sing the 'Five little ducks' song together, taking one duck away. Ask 'How many are left now?'

- Repeat the activity.

PLENARY

Place all five ducks back into the pond, sing the song one last time and as the ducks swim away place them into the finish box.

CONSOLIDATION ACTIVITY

The same game can be played with five little monkeys, five little frogs or any other counting game. As the child's experience grows, you could add a mark-making element by their writing the number on a whiteboard to correlate with the number of animals selected.

62. Bounce that Ball!

Learning Objective

P8 pupils join in with counting by rote to beyond ten.

Additional Skills

Visual: following a moving object at the same time as counting.

Tactile: feeling different textured balls.

Social communication: working as part of a small group.

Gross motor: bouncing a ball.

Resources

A range of different textured balls in a box

Laminated 'more' and 'less' symbols

Laminated action symbols

MAIN

- Working in a small group, ask the children to sit in a semicircle.
- The adult models feeling the different textured balls and choosing one.
- The adult stands in front of the group and bounces the ball as many times as possible, counting as they go and encouraging the others to join in.
- Choose a child to come to the front and choose a ball.
- Encourage the child to bounce the ball, counting as they go.
- When the child has finished, ask the group if the child bounced the ball 'more' or 'less' times than the adult.
- Ask the child to choose a friend to come and have a turn.
- Encourage all the children to watch their friends and join in with counting by rote beyond ten.

PLENARY

Choose a child to come to the front of the group. Ask them to choose an action symbol and then ask them to do the action as many times as they can before they are too tired! Encourage everyone to count along with the child's action. Repeat with the other children and ask each time whether they did an action 'more' or 'less' times than their friends.

CONSOLIDATION ACTIVITY

On different playground equipment encourage the child to count by rote beyond ten; for example, count how many times the roundabout goes around, count pushes on the swing or count how many large strides it takes to cross the playground.

63. Count On Me

Learning Objective

P8 pupils continue to count by rote onwards from a given small number.

Additional Skills

Kinaesthetic: moving along the ladder/snake shape.

Social communication: working with partners and as part of a group.

Auditory: listening to instructions from a peer.

Resources

Chalk

Playground surface

Large dice

Action symbols

Laminated '10' symbol

MAIN

- On the playground use chalk to draw out a giant ladder or snake shape with numbers in the boxes.

- Ask child A to roll the dice and call out the number.

- Child B goes and stands on that number.

- Child A rolls the dice again and child B moves the amount along the shape.

- Repeat until child B reaches the end of the ladder/ snake shape and then ask them to swap roles.

- Once the children are familiar with the activity, ask more children to join and turn the game into a race to the finish line!

PLENARY

The child chooses an action symbol then rolls the dice. The adult holds up the laminated '10' symbol. Count with the child, doing the action up to the amount on the dice and then encourage them to carry on counting and doing the action up to ten.

CONSOLIDATION ACTIVITY

Count in everyday situations, such as counting how many children are in the class or how many chairs are needed at a table. The adult should start the child counting and then encourage them to carry on counting up to ten objects in any given situation.

64. Cake Quantity

Learning Objective

P8 pupils recognise differences in quantity.

Additional Skills

Visual: recognising differences in quantity.

Social communication: waiting a turn and working as part of a group.

Kinaesthetic: arm movements to splat the foam cakes.

Resources

Cake cases

Shaving foam or play foam

Builder's tray

Laminated 'more', 'less', 'bigger', 'smaller' symbols

Two trays

Two tea towels/cloths

Range of small world toys, for example zoo or farm animals

MAIN

- The adult sets up the builder's tray with two cake cases in front of the child.
- Spray the foam into both cake cases, making one a bit bigger than the other.
- Ask the child 'Which one has more/less/is bigger/smaller?' and encourage them to indicate the answer using gesture, symbol or speech.
- Add more cake cases and make a group with big 'cakes' and a group with smaller 'cakes'.
- Again ask the child to indicate 'Which one has more/less/is bigger/smaller?'
- Ask the child which group we should 'splat' first – encourage the child to come up and splat the cakes in the group they have chosen.

PLENARY

Place different amounts of small world toys on the two different trays and cover them with the tea towels. Make a show of removing the towels to reveal the different trays and ask the children to indicate which tray has more or less toys or is the bigger or smaller group. Repeat a couple of times with different amounts each time, sometimes making the differences more or less obvious.

CONSOLIDATION ACTIVITY

In the playground, encourage the children to play a game where an adult counts to five and then the children choose to run to a choice of two different areas. Encourage the children to identify which group is bigger/smaller or has more or less children in it.

65. My Guess Is Seven

Learning Objective

P8 pupils estimate a small number and then check it by counting.

Additional Skills

Communication: making an estimate using voice or sign.

Attention: engaging for over 15 minutes.

Tactile: using tactile discrimination skills to find objects out of sight.

Resources

Large box

Sensory materials (shredded paper, rice, tinsel, pasta, sand, etc.)

Ten cars (or favourite toys)

Whiteboard and pens

Finish box

MAIN

- Create a sensory tub filled with the sensory material. Have a collection of ten cars (or ten of the child's favourite items).

- With the child watching, hide a selection of these in the sensory tub and place the others out of sight.

- Ask the child to estimate how many cars got put into the sensory tub.

- The adult and child should write an estimate on a whiteboard.

- The child then explores in the sensory tub and tries to find them all. Count them as they are returned to the adult. Was the estimate correct?

- Repeat the activity, with the adult and child taking turns to estimate.

PLENARY

Hide all ten items in the box and then the child counts them into the finish box.

CONSOLIDATION ACTIVITY

Hide some treasure in the sand tray and repeat the same steps as in the main activity.

66. What's My Numeral?

Learning Objective

P8 pupils recognise numerals from one to nine and relate them to sets of objects.

Additional Skills

Social communication: turn taking.

Gross motor: aiming and rolling balls.

Fine motor: writing numerals.

Resources

Set of skittles or ten empty drink bottles

Two small balls

'1'–'9' laminated number cards

Whiteboard and pen

MAIN

- Set up the skittles and two balls with a set of laminated number cards, a whiteboard and a pen ready for the activity to start.

- Ask the child to count how many skittles there are and show you the number.

- Roll one ball and ask 'How many are there left now?' Show the correct numeral and write this on the whiteboard.

- Roll the second ball and ask 'How many are left?' Show the numeral.

- The adult should keep an overall running tally of the points scored to model how to do this, with the child adding each time.

- Repeat the activity with the adult taking turns or a small group of peers.

PLENARY

Each child has one last turn – they are asked to predict how many skittles they will knock down and select a number card to reflect this. Take turns and count to see if the prediction was correct.

CONSOLIDATION ACTIVITY

Set this game up in the playground with bottles filled with sand and a small football. Practise kicking and aiming skills by attempting to knock down the skittles.

67. Who's First?

Learning Objective

P8 pupils use ordinal numbers when describing the position of things.

Additional Skills

Social communication: turn taking.

Fine motor: activating toys and scissor skills.

Communication: indicating through voice or sign who is first, second and third.

Resources

Self-propelling toys (pull-and-go cars, bugs, wind-up toys, etc.)

Card

Scissors

Coloured pens

Ribbon

Chalk to mark out a start and finish line

Finish box

MAIN

- Collect together a set of three self-propelling toys or objects and set up a racetrack.

- Before you play with these, tell the child that there is going to be a race and medals need to be made.

- Create a set of first, second and third medals and a podium if you are feeling creative.

- Once the medals are ready, set up the race.

- The adult may need to control one or two of the items, depending upon the child's motor skills.

- Ready, steady, go! Who crosses the finish line first?

- Have an awards ceremony where each object receives their medal and a clap. Repeat the activity.

PLENARY

Set up the finish box at the end of the track and have a race to see which toy makes it into the box first.

CONSOLIDATION ACTIVITY

If you have the option to take the child out to look at ordinal numbers in the environment, this would support their understanding. Examples of this would be an electronic bus timetable at the bus stop, a train timetable, an airport lounge or a ticket at the counter in the supermarket. Alternatively, as you ask the children to line up for lunch, the adult can use ordinal numbers.

SHAPE, SPACE AND MEASURE

68. Watch Me Go

Learning Objective

P4 pupils search for objects that have gone out of sight, hearing or touch, demonstrating the beginning of object permanence.

Additional Skills

Visual: tracking the movement of an object.

Attention: focusing on activity for up to two minutes.

Fine motor: posting objects into a tube.

Tactile: experiencing different messy media.

Resources

Long cardboard tube

Cars or light-up sensory balls (or other objects the child finds motivating)

Box with water or dry messy media, depending on the child's preference

MAIN

- Show the child the car/sensory ball.
- Place the car/sensory ball at the top of the tube and say 'Ready, steady, go!'
- Encourage the child to watch the car/sensory ball go into the tube and watch for it to splash into the box at the end of the tube.
- Encourage the child to find the car/sensory ball in the water/dry messy media and return it to the adult to repeat the activity.

PLENARY

Encourage the child to take a turn posting the object into the tube and finding the object again to repeat the activity.

CONSOLIDATION ACTIVITY

In the playground or at other playtimes find an object the child finds motivating and show it to the child in your hand. The adult places their hands behind their back and encourages the child to find the object.

69. Big Teddy, Small Teddy

Learning Objective

P4 pupils match big objects and small objects.

Additional Skills

Visual: noticing the marked difference in size between objects.

Kinaesthetic: moving to match teddies.

Auditory: listening to verbal instructions.

Social communication: tolerating spending time doing a shared activity.

Resources

A range of big and small teddies

A very big teddy

A very small teddy

Laminated 'big' and 'small' symbols

Two boxes

A range of cutlery items – both big and small, for example a big and small plate and spoon

MAIN

- The adult and child sit together at a table or on the carpet.
- The adult brings out the big teddy and uses minimal language to describe it as the big teddy to the child.
- Place the teddy on the table/carpet with the 'big' symbol in front.
- Repeat for the small teddy.
- The adult shows the child the different big and small teddies.
- Explore them together. The adult supports the child to match, for example, the small teddy to the small teddy and symbol.
- Repeat for all the teddies.
- As the child gets more familiar with the activity, encourage them to be as independent as possible while matching the teddies.

PLENARY

Place the big teddy and 'big' symbol in one box and the small teddy and 'small' symbol in the other box. Ask the child to tidy up the activity by matching the teddies to the correct box.

CONSOLIDATION ACTIVITY

Set up the big and small teddies at a table or 'picnic'. Ask the child to give, for example, the big spoon to the big teddy or the small plate to the small teddy. At P4 you will need to hand the child the correct object, as opposed to them finding the big spoon or small plate from a range of objects themselves.

70. Box It

Learning Objective

P4 pupils demonstrate an interest in position and the relationship between objects.

Additional Skills

Tactile: feeling the texture and size of different boxes.

Gross motor: building with large boxes.

Kinaesthetic: pushing the tower over.

Fine motor: using scissors and tape as construction materials.

Resources

A large range of different-sized cardboard boxes

Tape and scissors (if you want to extend the activity)

Ball

MAIN

- Set up boxes on the carpet or a corner of the classroom so that they look plentiful and inviting to play with.

- The adult models building a tower with the boxes, sometimes getting it wrong, for example putting a large box on a small box. The adult also models rotating the boxes to stand them on different sides.

- When a tower has been made, shout 'One, two, three, go!' and push the tower over.

- Encourage the child to build their own tower using as many of the boxes as possible and then pushing them over.

Teaching note: if the child is able, use scissors to cut tape then tape some of the boxes together in different positions. Try building something other than a tower, like a pirate ship or house.

PLENARY

Set up the boxes again in three towers this time, and throw a ball at each tower, seeing who can knock it down first!

CONSOLIDATION ACTIVITY

Take the boxes into the playground and encourage the child to join in with other children's play as they use the boxes to build different imaginative scenes.

71. Can You Find It?

Learning Objective

P4 pupils search for objects that have gone out of sight, hearing or touch, demonstrating the beginning of object permanence.

Additional Skills

Tactile: exploring textures and toys.

Fine motor: opening boxes and containers.

Social communication: sharing an experience.

Resources

Builder's tray

Different-size boxes

Different-size containers (screw lids, pop lids, etc.)

Sensory toys (spinning tops, flashing balls, vibrating items, wind-up toys)

Massage cream

Music

MAIN

- Set up the builder's tray on the table with lots of different boxes and containers.

- Using the selection of sensory toys, hide all of these in the different boxes.

- Allow the child time to begin exploring the tray. If they have not noticed any of the items, shake one of the containers.

- When the child finds an item, spend time exploring this with them, put it into the finish box and say and sign 'more' to indicate they should continue searching.

PLENARY

Put on some relaxing music and have a hand massage to finish the activity.

CONSOLIDATION ACTIVITY

Repeat this activity with different items (musical instruments, snack items, etc.) so that they begin to understand object permanence.

72. Who Left It Out?

Learning Objective

P4 pupils match big and small objects.

Additional Skills

Social communication: team working.

Visual: matching a photo to an object.

Kinaesthetic: running and collecting objects.

Auditory: listening to instructions.

Resources

Footballs

Tennis balls

Tennis rackets

Cones

Hockey sticks

Large bags or boxes

Photos of each item

Stopwatch

MAIN

- Set up all the equipment in the playground.

- Tell the group of children that someone has left all of the PE equipment outside and it needs sorting.

- Split the children into groups.

- Hand each of the groups a photo of the object that they need to collect.

- Ensure that the children who need the constant visual prompts are holding the photos.

- Set the stopwatch to see how long everyone takes. 'Ready, steady, go!'

PLENARY

Carry all the bags back to the PE cupboard; heavy work can help to regulate the sensory systems.

CONSOLIDATION ACTIVITY

A similar activity can be done in class by sorting out the art equipment on a one-to-one basis, without photos. Use the real objects instead of photos; for example, show the child a paintbrush and support them in finding more paintbrushes.

73. Tumbling Towers

Learning Objective

P4 pupils demonstrate an interest in position and the relationship between objects.

Additional Skills

Attention: building anticipation and waiting.

Communication: using 'go' as a cue for action.

Gross motor: building and knocking down towers.

Social communication: enjoying spending time with a familiar adult.

Resources

Construction set

Builder's tray

Finish box

MAIN

- On the builder's tray, set up a construction set in towers of varying heights.

- Build anticipation with the child by saying 'Ready, steady, go!' and then knocking a tower down. Repeat this for all the towers.

- When everything has been knocked down, begin building a tower and then pass the next block to the child to add.

- Build a tower, then say 'Ready, steady, go!' and the child can knock it down.

- Repeat this by building as many towers as the child can wait for or as high as you can make them.

PLENARY

Make one last really tall tower in the finish box. Knock this down. Place the rest of the pieces into the box.

CONSOLIDATION ACTIVITY

Read the story 'The Three Little Pigs'. Gather different types of construction material and make different towers, telling the story as you go. Replace 'Ready, steady, go!' for 'I huff and I puff and I blow the house down!'

74. Setting-Up Skills

Learning Objective

P5 pupils search intentionally for objects in their usual place.

Additional Skills

Auditory: responding to verbal instructions.

Kinaesthetic: moving around the classroom.

Visual: matching objects to pictures.

Attention: being able to move around the room and then focus on the activity.

Resources

Symbol/photo of familiar activity (e.g. painting)

Photos of the resources needed for the activity (e.g. paintbrush, paint, water pot, paper)

MAIN

- Show child the photo of the familiar activity, for example painting.

- The adult explains that they forgot to get the things needed for painting!

- Ask the child to help set up the activity.

- Show the child the photo of the resources needed, for example a paintbrush, and ask them to find it and bring it back to the table.

- Repeat this for, for example, the paper and paint.

- Thank the child for finding everything needed for painting and then engage them in the activity.

Teaching note: to help the child to find the resources to start with, put photos around the classroom where they are kept as a visual prompt. Once they know where they are kept, remove the photos.

PLENARY

Ask the child to tidy up the activity by returning all the resources to the correct place.

CONSOLIDATION ACTIVITY

When the child is familiar with this routine for one activity, repeat it for other activities.

75. Post It

Learning Objective

P5 pupils find big and small objects on request.

Additional Skills

Auditory: listening to verbal instructions.

Tactile: feeling the different sizes of objects.

Visual: tracking an object from one end of the tube to the other.

Social communication: responding to requests made by a peer.

Resources

Big and small cardboard tube

Big and small balls (that fit down the tubes)

One big box

One small box

Laminated 'big' and 'small' symbols

A range of other big and small objects

MAIN

• Have all the resources mixed up on the table but in groups, i.e. the tubes together, the boxes together and the balls together.

• Ask the child to find the big tube and identify it using symbols or speech.

• Ask the child to find the big box.

• Ask the child to find the big ball and post it down the big tube into the big box.

• Repeat for the small resources.

• Bring out the range of other big and small objects.

• Make the activity more challenging by, for example, asking the child to find the big tube, the small box and the big car.

PLENARY

Encourage the child to choose a friend to come and play the game. The friend takes the place of the adult and makes requests for the big and small objects. If appropriate, the children then swap roles.

CONSOLIDATION ACTIVITY

At snack or lunchtimes ask the child to, for example, find the big spoon or sit on the small chair.

76. Sandcastle Space

Learning Objective

P5 pupils explore the position of objects.

Additional Skills

Fine motor: filling and emptying containers.

Tactile: exploring different sensory media.

Visual: noticing the position of objects.

Communication: answering a question.

Resources

Builder's tray

Sand

Water spray

Big and small containers

Big and small spoons

Laminated 'big' and 'small' symbols

MAIN

- Place the big and small containers in the builder's tray and, with the child, identify which ones are big and small using symbols or speech.

- Show the child the tub of sand and ask them to use the big or small spoon to fill up a big container, fitting in as much sand as possible.

- Spray the sand to make it damp and turn the container over to make a sandcastle.

- Ask the child to use a big or small spoon to fill up a small container, spray it with water and make a sandcastle next to the first.

- Compare the sizes. Which one is bigger? Which one is smaller?

- Repeat the activity with even bigger and even smaller containers and encourage the child to think about where there is enough space in the tray to make the sandcastle, thinking about the position of the container.

PLENARY

When the child has set out all the sandcastles possible in the tray, ask them to identify which ones are small and which ones are big, using symbols or speech. Then splat all the sandcastles, put all the sand back in the tub and repeat the activity.

CONSOLIDATION ACTIVITY

This activity could be repeated in the sand tray or outside using different sensory media such as flour.

77. Boxing Clever

Learning Objective

P5 pupils compare the overall size of one object with that of another where there is a marked difference.

Additional Skills

Gross motor: squashing the teddies into the boxes.

Social communication: working as part of a small group.

Tactile: feeling the marked difference in size of boxes.

Kinaesthetic: climbing in and out of boxes.

Resources

A range of boxes of different sizes (with at least one the child could fit into)

A range of different-size toys such as teddies

MAIN

- Show the child the range of different-size boxes.

- Ask 'How many teddies can we get into the big box?' and model placing as many teddies as possible into the big box.

- Repeat for the different sizes, encouraging the child to join in.

- Encourage the child to notice that, as the boxes get smaller, fewer teddies fit in.

- Encourage the child to explore the different-sized boxes through independently trying to fit as many teddies or other objects into the boxes.

PLENARY

Encourage the child to explore the different-size boxes by seeing if they can fit themselves into the boxes! Which one is big enough? 'How much of you can fit in the smallest box?'

CONSOLIDATION ACTIVITY

Encourage other children to come and join the game, seeing who can fit into which box. Maybe have a box big enough for several children to get in and one that only a little finger can fit in.

78. Big Teddy Wants a Big Bowl

Learning Objective

P5 pupils find big and small objects on request.

Additional Skills

Social communication: working together.

Kinaesthetic: moving the resources around.

Visual: noticing big and small.

Auditory: listening to the story.

Resources

Basket

Finish box

Big teddy

Small teddy

Big and small bowl, spoon, chair and bed/ blanket

Book: 'Goldilocks and the Three Bears'

MAIN

- Have all the resources prepared in a basket.
- Read the story of 'Goldilocks and the Three Bears'.
- Ask the child to give the big teddy the big bowl.
- Repeat until the big and small teddies have all the resources they need.
- Act out the story together using the resources, key words and sounds.

PLENARY

Put all the resources into the finish box and put the big and small teddies to bed.

CONSOLIDATION ACTIVITY

Act out the story with the adult being the big teddy and the child the small teddy. Ask other children to be the middle-size teddy and Goldilocks.

79. If the Shoe Fits

Learning Objective

P5 pupils compare the overall size of one object with that of another where there is a marked difference.

Additional Skills

Fine motor: shoelaces and fastenings.

Communication: responding to clues and prompts.

Attention: focusing for over seven minutes.

Social communication: working as part of a large group.

Resources

Nothing additional

MAIN

- All the children and adults sit in a large circle.

- Everyone in the group (children and adults) takes their shoes off and places them in the middle of the circle.

- One child at a time is asked to find the shoes of another person.

- For the child who may find this tricky, wait until a few have been chosen already and then ask them to find adult shoes.

- If the shoes cannot be found, ask the owner for some clues.

- Repeat in the group until everyone has their shoes back.

PLENARY

Once everyone has their shoes back, allow the children plenty of time to try and independently put them on and do them up.

CONSOLIDATION ACTIVITY

The same activity could be carried out with coats.

80. Let's Find It

Learning Objective

P5 pupils search intentionally for objects in their usual place.

Additional Skills

Visual: looking at photos.

Attention: focusing for over five minutes.

Communication: key words or pointing at pictures.

Resources

Map of the classroom

Laminated photos of small common classroom items (pencil, paintbrush, cup, teddy, book, etc.)

Bag

MAIN

- Place the map of the classroom and the visual cue cards into a bag.
- Show the bag to the child and say you need to fill the bag with the items for the teacher to help with her lesson.
- Look at the map and, using single words only, say what is in each area: 'art', 'maths', 'books', etc.
- Pull out a picture card, look at it and name the item.
- Show the child the map and ask where they should look.
- Go to that area and when you find the item place it in the bag.
- Work through all the picture cards.

PLENARY

When the activity has finished, the child present the bag to the teacher.

CONSOLIDATION ACTIVITY

Plan a similar activity for outside and ask classmates to join in so that the adult can gradually decrease their support.

81. Squash It In

Learning Objective

P5 pupils explore the position of objects.

Additional Skills

Fine motor: manipulating clothes and fastenings.

Gross motor: squashing items in to a backpack.

Social communication: working together.

Communication: making decisions.

Resources

Backpack

Dressing-up box

Access to an atlas

MAIN

• Show the child a clip of a person packing to go on holiday.

• Tell the child that the adult needs to pack to go on holiday for the weekend.

• Present the child with a backpack and the dressing-up box.

• Explore the clothes together and try lots of things on.

• When you both decide the item would be good to take, ask the child to put this in the backpack.

• Keep going until it is hard to fit anything else in, so that the child needs to problem solve. For example: Are there any pockets that could be used? Does the snorkel need to be packed?

PLENARY

Put the backpack on and go to the library. Have a look at an atlas together and decide where in the world you could go.

CONSOLIDATION ACTIVITY

The next time the class is going on a trip, create a list and ask the child to pack the items in the class backpack.

82. Hide and Seek

Learning Objective

P6 pupils search for objects not found in their usual place, demonstrating their understanding of object permanence.

Additional Skills

Communication: using gesture or speech to indicate that something is missing.

Social communication: recognising a familiar adult.

Kinaesthetic: moving around the school.

Resources

The cooperation of colleagues!

Photos of colleagues

A map of the school with rooms of familiar people marked

MAIN

- Before the lesson ask some colleagues if they could play a game of hide and seek! For example, ask the receptionist, deputy head, school nurse, etc. if they could go and hide in a different room.

- Show the child a photo of one of the familiar adults who has agreed to hide.

- Ask them to go and find them.

- When they are not in their usual office, encourage the child to think of other places they might be.

- Use the map to hunt around the school for the familiar person.

PLENARY

Encourage the child to choose a friend to come and play hide and seek in the playground.

CONSOLIDATION ACTIVITY

At familiar times of the day such as playtime, home time, etc. place familiar objects such as the child's coat or bag in a different place and encourage them to hunt and find it.

83. Size Matters

Learning Objective

P6 pupils compare the overall size of one object with that of another where the difference is not great.

Additional Skills

Fine motor: scissor skills.

Visual: recognising difference in size where the difference is not great.

Social communication: working as part of a group.

Communication: giving instructions to peers.

Resources

Pre-made hand or footprints

Laminated 'biggest' and 'smallest' symbols

MAIN

- In a previous lesson encourage a small group or whole class to make hand or footprints.

- In this lesson encourage the child to choose several different hand or footprints and use scissors to cut them out.

- The adult places the 'biggest' symbol at one end of the table and the 'smallest' symbol at the other end of the table.

- Encourage the child to place one hand/footprint over the other to compare the size, and with support arrange them from biggest to smallest along the table.

- The order will probably change a few times as the child keeps comparing the hand/footprints.

PLENARY

The children work in a small group. Ask the children to line up and then ask the child to indicate who the biggest is and who the smallest is. The child works with a partner to arrange the children from biggest to smallest.

CONSOLIDATION ACTIVITY

During different activities such as colouring or snack times ask the child to compare the different sizes of, for example, the pencils or the fruits and indicate which is the smallest or the biggest.

84. Position Me

Learning Objective

P6 pupils show an understanding of words, signs and symbols that describe positions.

Additional Skills

Gross motor: throwing large dice.

Kinaesthetic: moving according to position symbol.

Social communication: turn taking.

Communication: receptive understanding of instructions.

Resources

Two large dice

Six objects such as a chair, carpet, blanket, box, step, cushion (some can be repeated)

Symbols of objects stuck to one of the dice

Six symbols of position instructions, for example including 'next to', 'on top', 'under', 'in' (some can be repeated)

These symbols stuck on the faces of the other dice

MAIN

- The children sit in a small group in a wide semicircle with objects set up in the middle.

- The adult models rolling the first dice and identifies the object, for example the blanket.

- The adult models rolling the second dice and then follows the instruction, for example crawling under the blanket.

- Encourage children to take turns with the activity.

- Do all the instructions work? Can you climb in (rather than on) the chair?

- Encourage the children to help each other verbally by offering suggestions, for example 'Roll the dice again!'

PLENARY

Ask the children to tidy away all the objects, using instructions such as 'Can you put the chair next to the table?'

CONSOLIDATION ACTIVITY

Throughout the day encourage the child to respond to positional language; for example, when lining up for the playground ask them to stand next to a particular person or object. In the playground encourage them, for example, to hide under the slide.

85. Who Moved It?

Learning Objective

P6 pupils search for objects not found in their usual place, demonstrating their understanding of object permanence.

Additional Skills

Attention: persisting with a task for over seven minutes.

Social communication: working together.

Visual: searching for and locating items.

Resources

Map of the classroom

Photos of familiar classroom items (paintbrush, cup, book, scissors, etc.)

Bag

MAIN

- Prior to the lesson move all the classroom items into different places.
- Using the map that was created in P5 for 'Let's Find It' (Lesson 80) and the photos, ask the child to collect all the items that the teacher needs in the bag.
- When getting to the first familiar place (at the cupboard for paintbrushes) the adult should be shocked that there are no art supplies there: 'What can we do? Where can we look?'
- Go on a hunt together around the classroom, looking for where the art supplies may be.
- When selecting the next photo, ask the child to think about where they usually are, using the map of the class, and whether they have already seen them this morning.
- Keep working through all the photos until the resources are collected and placed in the bag.

PLENARY

The child should go and find the teacher and show them that all the items they wanted have been found.

CONSOLIDATION ACTIVITY

The child could hide items in the class to challenge a classmate to find.

86. Hook It Out

Learning Objective

P6 pupils compare the overall size of one object with that of another where the difference is not great.

Additional Skills

Hand–eye coordination: using the fishing rod.

Auditory: listening to verbal instructions.

Visual: noticing differences in shape.

Resources

Paper cut-outs of fish, ducks and frogs of different sizes (small, medium, large) – there needs to be variance between the sizes of all the creatures to meet the target

Paperclips – attach one to each of the cut-out creatures

Stick with string and a magnet on the end (fishing rod)

Builder's tray

Finish box

MAIN

- Set up the builder's tray with all the cut-out animals.

- Hand the child the fishing rod and ask them to find two small fish, then three medium frogs, etc.

- Continue until all the animals have been fished out of the 'pond'.

PLENARY

Use the fishing rod to place all the creatures into the finish box.

CONSOLIDATION ACTIVITY

Hide metal items in the sand tray and ask the child to find two medium items using the fishing rod, then one small item, etc.

87. Push It

Learning Objective

P6 pupils manipulate 3D shapes.

Additional Skills

Social communication: team working.

Gross motor: manipulating large items.

Kinaesthetic: pushing and pulling large items.

Auditory: listening to instructions.

Resources

Therapy balls

Tennis balls

Cardboard box

Cones

Ramp (if available)

MAIN

- Set up a course in the hall with ramps and cones.
- Split the children into teams.
- Provide each team with a large therapy ball.
- Model to them pushing the ball around the course. 'Ready, steady, go!'
- Now give the children a tennis ball – can they manoeuvre this around the course?
- Last, use a large cardboard box.
- At the end of the races, ask the children which was the easiest to take around the course.

PLENARY

Do stretches to cool down from the PE session.

CONSOLIDATION ACTIVITY

Set up a course with cones in the playground. Give each team a hockey stick and a box of items (ball, beanbag, ice cream box, etc.) that they need to push around the course.

88. Where Shall I Go?

Learning Objective

P6 pupils show an understanding of words, signs and symbols that describe positions.

Additional Skills

Visual: looking at the instruction cards.

Social communication: being part of a group.

Attention: engaging for longer than ten minutes.

Kinaesthetic: moving around the space.

Communication: understanding and responding to instructions.

Resources

Position cards ('on', 'under', 'next to', 'behind', 'in front of')

Photos of locations or objects

Blankets and other items to create variance if there are limited places to move in the setting

Finish box

MAIN

- In one hand hold the position cards; in the other have the location.
- Tell all the children in the group to look closely at all the cards and then pick two cards to show them.
- The children need to look at the cards and follow the actions (e.g. 'behind' 'tree', 'under' 'blanket').
- Repeat a few times.
- Ask a child to take a turn at giving instructions to the group.
- Do all of the actions work? Can we go on top of the tree?

PLENARY

Gather all the equipment and place it in the finish box.

CONSOLIDATION ACTIVITY

This game can be played in a variety of school locations; some of the location cards will need to be changed.

89. What's in the Heavy Box?

Learning Objective

P7 pupils use familiar words in practical situations when they compare sizes and quantities.

Additional Skills

Kinaesthetic: responding to 'heavy' and 'light'.

Visual: searching the room for items.

Tactile: exploring sensory items.

Communication: identifying 'heavy' and 'light'.

Social communication: asking a classmate to join with the activity and working together.

Resources

Identical boxes or tubs

Selection of materials to make boxes heavy/light (rice, cotton wool, bubbles, pasta, pencils, stones, glitter, etc.)

Symbols for 'heavy' and 'light'

Electronic tablet with a heavy and light video clip prepared

MAIN

- Have the boxes set up in a row along the table.
- Show the child a clip about 'heavy' and 'light' on the tablet.
- Ask the child to find you a heavy box.
- When the child hands it to you, exaggerate the heavy or light aspect.
- Once the child has explored the weight of all the objects and used comparative language or symbols, open the boxes.
- Spend time with the child exploring the materials.
- Can they find an item in the class to make a heavy box? Repeat this with a light box.

PLENARY

Ask the child to choose a classmate and see if they can identify the heavy and light boxes that they have just put together.

CONSOLIDATION ACTIVITY

Add coloured water to different-size bottles and repeat the activity. This means the focus is on the feeling of 'heavy' and 'light', rather than the appearance.

90. Paint by Shapes

Learning Objective

P7 pupils pick out described shapes from a collection.

Additional Skills

Visual: noticing shapes within a picture.

Fine motor: holding a pencil or paintbrush in a tripod grip.

Auditory: listening to instructions.

Social communication: accepting support from an adult.

Resources

2D geometric shape kit

White paper

Art book

Paint/crayons

MAIN

• The adult shows the children a book of paintings by artists from around the world.

• Look through this together and find a picture that the child particularly likes.

• Talk together about what shapes you can see in the picture.

• Ask the child to choose 2D geometric shapes from the picture and place them on the white paper. Keep going until the painting is represented.

• On separate pieces of paper, both the adult and child should begin to draw the shapes that the child has identified.

• Once this is complete, select the appropriate colours (paint/crayons) to add colour to the painting.

PLENARY

The child should write their own name and, with support, the original artist and the title of the painting. Place this in the class gallery.

CONSOLIDATION ACTIVITY

This activity can be linked to the class topic or story. Look at the pictures or objects and recreate them using the geometric shapes.

91. Forward to the Winning Line

Learning Objective

P7 pupils respond to 'forwards' and 'backwards'.

Additional Skills

Social communication: working with others, following conventional rules.

Fine motor: tripod pen grip.

Auditory: listening to instructions.

Resources

Large paper

Felt tip pens

Dice

Place markers

MAIN

- Set out a large piece of paper on the table or floor with a selection of felt tip pens.
- Create a track together. Your aim is to create a snakes-and-ladders-type game. If the child has a specific interest, such as cars or trains, tailor the track to meet their interest.
- Fill out the numbers on the track together.
- Add the move forwards (ladders) and move backwards (snakes) options.
- Roll the dice to see who goes first.
- Play the game together; invite classmates to join the game.

PLENARY

Fold up the paper and find a box where all the pieces can go so that it can be played again.

CONSOLIDATION ACTIVITY

Take the game outside on a sunny day. Ask the child to approach peers to see if they would like to play. The adult takes an observation approach rather than leading the game.

92. Mapping Movements

Learning Objective

P7 pupils respond to 'forwards' and 'backwards'.

Additional Skills

Auditory: listening to verbal instructions.

Social communication: working as part of a small group and turn taking.

Fine motor: using big chalks for drawing.

Kinaesthetic: moving according to instructions.

Resources

Large chalks

Laminated position symbols

Laminated number cards '0'–'5'

MAIN

- The children should work in small groups of three to four, with support where appropriate.

- Children A and B should use large chalks to draw a road on the playground floor that includes a change of direction.

- Children C and D should stand at the beginning of the road and act like robots, only responding to instructions given by children A and B.

- Children A and B should direct classmates around their road to the end using positional language.

- Swap roles and repeat. Extend the activity by adding places to get to, for example the fire station.

PLENARY

All the children line up. The adult holds up a number card and then a forwards or backwards symbol, and the children count as they move forwards or backwards.

CONSOLIDATION ACTIVITY

Throughout the day, for example when lining up or coming to sit in the circle, encourage children to move forwards or backwards from their position.

93. Fish Out a Shape

Learning Objective

P7 pupils pick out described shapes from a collection.

Additional Skills

Social communication: working in partners.

Communication: understanding and describing different shapes.

Tactile: feeling different shapes.

Fine motor: using a fishing net or scoop to fish out the shapes.

Resources

Box of mixed 2D or 3D shapes

Water tray

Fishing nets (or some kind of scoop)

Laminated shape symbols

Laminated symbols to support the shape description

MAIN

- The adult shakes up the box of shapes and shouts 'One, two, three, go!' and empties the box into the water tray.

- The adult then uses symbols to support sentences such as 'Find the shape with three sides'.

- The child uses the fishing net to scoop out the shape and match it to the appropriate laminated shape card.

- Repeat for all the shapes.

- When the child is familiar with the activity encourage them to choose a friend to come and play the game with them, swapping roles so that they have to describe the shape as well as find it.

Teaching note: initially, to build up their understanding of descriptive shape language, it may be best to ask the child to find the shape and then look at its characteristics together, for example asking them to find a triangle and then showing them that it has three sides.

PLENARY

The adult asks the child to tidy up by describing or naming the shapes so the child can find the shapes to put back in the box.

CONSOLIDATION ACTIVITY

In the playground or in free times throughout the day, the adult or a classmates describes a shape to the child and they try to draw it using a whiteboard and pen. The adult or peer swaps roles so that the child describes the shape for their partner.

94. Water Weights

Learning Objective

P7 pupils use familiar words in practical situations when they compare sizes and quantities.

Additional Skills

Tactile: exploring objects in the water.

Communication: using and understanding familiar words.

Gross motor: dropping objects into the water.

Auditory: understanding verbal instructions.

Resources

Water tray

Range of heavy and light objects

Empty plastic bottles

Laminated 'heavy', 'light', 'more' and 'less' symbols

MAIN

- At the water tray encourage the child to feel and compare different weights, for example a potato versus a feather, and then match them to the 'heavy' and 'light' symbols.

- Once there is a pile of heavy and light objects ask the child to find, for example, a heavy object and drop it into the water. Talk about what happens.

- Repeat for the light object.

- Repeat until all the objects have been dropped into the water tray.

- Encourage the child to talk about the difference between the heavy and light objects.

PLENARY

Explore the water bottles in the water tray. The adult fills the bottle to the top and asks the child to put less water in their bottle. Swap roles and continue to play the game.

CONSOLIDATION ACTIVITY

In practical situations throughout the day ask the child to bring you different objects such as a chair or a pencil and ask them if the object was heavy or light. Also at snack or lunchtimes ask the child: Who has more or less on their plates? and generally encourage conversation that requires the child to answer using familiar words such as 'heavy', 'light', 'more', 'less', enough' or 'not enough'.

95. Snap – My Shape Has Four Straight Sides

Learning Objective

P8 pupils describe shapes in simple models, pictures and patterns.

Additional Skills

Communication: describing a feature of a shape.

Visual: noticing when two pictures are the same.

Fine motor: dealing and handling cards.

Resources

Shape snap cards

Counters

Access to board games

MAIN

- Deal out the cards to each of the players.

- Tell the children that the person who wins is the one who is able to describe the shapes to their friends – they get a counter.

- Begin to play snap. When the two pictures match, the player needs to describe the shape without saying its name.

- If they do this correctly, then they get a counter (those with limited language could say the colour).

- Keep playing.

- The counters can then be used to play a game of the winning player's choice.

PLENARY

Each player chooses one card from the pack. They give clues to all the players about what is on their card, and the player who guesses correctly wins the card.

CONSOLIDATION ACTIVITY

During quiet time, the shape snap can be offered as a choice activity that the children can play without adult support.

96. My Week

Learning Objective

P8 pupils show awareness of time.

Additional Skills

Communication: talking about activities in the week.

Visual: ensuring the object is in the centre of the electronic tablet screen before taking a photo.

Fine motor: scissor skills and holding a pen.

Resources

Simple visual timetable for the child

Electronic tablet that can take photos

Access to a printer

Large paper

Glue

Scissors

Pens

MAIN

- Show the child a simple visual timetable of their week, highlighting one or two key events that separate the days (avoid lunchtimes, playtimes or other activities that happen every day).

- Go around the school with a tablet and take photos together of these events or objects – this could be PE, library and ICT.

- When you're back in class, print out the photos.

- Ask the child what they do on a Monday. Can they find the photo?

- Stick this down and write the day.

- Repeat – sometimes asking what they do on a day or what day they do an activity.

PLENARY

Place this in the child's workstation or near to their peg to make reference to.

CONSOLIDATION ACTIVITY

When waiting for activities, sing the 'Days of the week' song together.

97. The Longest Snake in Class

Learning Objective

P8 pupils compare objects directly, focusing on one dimension such as length or height where the difference is marked and can indicate 'the long one' or 'the tall one'.

Additional Skills

Auditory: listening to instructions.

Fine motor: manipulating play dough.

Visual: comparing lengths.

Resources

Home-made or pre-bought play dough

Laminated snake, caterpillar and worm heads (one for each person)

Stopwatch

MAIN

- Place the laminated snake head on the table.
- Show the child that the timer is going to be set for four minutes.
- Explain that the adult and child are going to have a race to see who can build the longest body out of small balls of play dough in the time.
- 'Ready, steady, go!'
- When the four minutes has finished, count up the number of balls in each snake.
- Place the laminated caterpillar head on the table. Explain that this time there are two minutes to make the body. 'Ready, steady, go!'
- Place the laminated worm head on the table. Explain that this time there are 30 seconds to make the body. 'Ready, steady, go!'
- Spend time comparing the length of the creatures. Out of all six, which is the longest? And which is the shortest?

PLENARY

Gather all the play dough into a ball and squash it into a box for next time.

CONSOLIDATION ACTIVITY

Using chalk on the playground, set a stopwatch and see how long a line can be drawn in ten seconds, five seconds, etc. Talk about the longest and the shortest.

98. Who Is the Tallest?

Learning Objective

P8 pupils compare objects directly, focusing on one dimension such as length or height where the difference is marked and can indicate 'the long one' or 'the tall one'.

Additional Skills

Visual: recognising different heights.

Tactile: exploring different sensory media.

Gross motor: using spades or other objects to hunt in the sand.

Social communication: working as part of a group.

Resources

A range of animals, either laminated or small world, with marked difference in height

Sand tray

Laminated 'tall' and 'short' symbols

MAIN

- In the sand tray hide all the different animals.

- Model hunting in the sand for two different animals. When you find them, model comparing height and then matching the tall one to the 'tall' symbol and short one to the 'short' symbol.

- Encourage the child to engage with the game, each time comparing the heights of the two animals found and matching them to the symbols.

PLENARY

The children sit in a small group. The adult chooses two children to come to the front and stand back to back. Ask the children to decide who the tallest is and who the shortest is using speech or symbols to indicate their answer. Allow the two volunteers to choose two friends to come and play next.

CONSOLIDATION ACTIVITY

When out in the community or the playground encourage the child to look at two objects, for example two buildings, and ask them to indicate which the tall one is and which the short one is, using symbols or speech.

99. Days of the Week

Learning Objective

P8 pupils show awareness of time through some familiarity with names of the days of the week and significant times in their day, such as meal times and bed times.

Additional Skills

Auditory: listening to a song and following verbal instructions.

Communication: using symbols to build a timetable.

Social communication: working with an adult and asking for help when needed.

Visual: matching a symbol to an activity.

Resources

Laminated days of the week

Laminated symbols of events in the child's routine from the week, for example 'swimming' and 'after-school club'.

Whiteboard and pen

MAIN

- The adult and child lay out days of the week in order while singing the days of the week song: 'Days of the week (clap, clap), days of the week (clap, clap), there's Monday and there's Tuesday, there's Wednesday and there's Thursday, there's Friday and there's Saturday and then there's Sunday!' (Sing to *The Addams Family* theme tune.)

- The adult mixes up the routine symbols and drops them on the table or the carpet.

- Ask the child to sort the routine symbols onto the days that they happen.

- When the child is familiar with the activity add more events from their week for them to sort onto the correct days.

PLENARY

Using a whiteboard and pen the child and adult write out the daily timetable for the day using symbols and mark making.

CONSOLIDATION ACTIVITY

On a daily basis, encourage the child to build their own (or class) visual timetable using symbols.

100. Shape Sprint

Learning Objective

P8 pupils respond to mathematical vocabulary such as 'straight', 'circle' and 'larger' to describe the shape and size of solids and flat shapes.

Additional Skills

Auditory: listen to verbal instructions.

Visual: recognising different shapes in different contexts.

Social communication: working as part of a group.

Communication: using mathematical vocabulary to describe shapes.

Resources

Large circular mats and straight-edged carpets or equivalent laminated shapes of varying sizes

Benches and circular PE equipment of varying sizes

Laminated 'straight', 'circle', 'small' and 'large' symbols

MAIN

- Set up the hall with the shapes in different areas.

- Work in a small group and ask the child to stand in the middle of the hall.

- The adult stands on each shape and shows the symbols to match the shape to support the child's understanding.

- The adult stands at the front of the group and shows the symbols, for example a large circle, and all the children run and find that shape.

- Repeat for the other shapes set up in the room.

Teaching note: as children become familiar with the activity, increase the complexity of the description of the shape, for example different-size cones.

PLENARY

At the end of the session, ask the children to lie down on their favourite shape and describe the shape to the group. Play relaxing music and encourage the children to make shapes with their arms and legs, for example moving their arms in a circle and putting their legs straight in the air.

CONSOLIDATION ACTIVITY

Throughout the day ask the child to find different-shaped and -sized objects, for example 'Can you find the larger cup?'

101. Shape Bingo

Learning Objective

P8 pupils describe shapes in simple models, pictures and patterns.

Additional Skills

Communication: using speech or symbols to describe shapes.

Social communication: working in small groups and with partners.

Tactile: feeling different shapes and objects.

Auditory: listening to a description.

Resources

Range of 2D or 3D shapes in a closed box (several of each shape) – include everyday items, for example milk cartons, biscuit tins, egg boxes (one box per group)

Shape bingo sheet – vary the amount of shapes on the sheet according to experience/ability, for example two/four shapes

Whiteboards and pens

MAIN

- The children should work in small groups of three to four, with support where appropriate.

- Child A closes their eyes, pulls out a shape from the box and tries to describe the shape using symbols or speech, for example 'It has three sides.'

- Children B, C, D (sat with their backs to child A) listen to the description. The first one to put their hand up and identify the shape correctly puts the shape on their bingo mat.

- Repeat until one learner has bingo!

- Swap roles and play again.

PLENARY

The children get into pairs and take a whiteboard and pen. They walk around the classroom and identify and draw one 2D or 3D shape per pair. They then come back to the carpet and share their shapes with their classmates.

CONSOLIDATION ACTIVITY

Take the pupils out to the playground and label 2D or 3D shapes using Post-its/printed shape images.

Claire Brewer has been teaching pupils with severe learning difficulties, profound and multiple learning difficulties and autism since completing her PGCE at Goldsmiths University. Claire holds a Masters in Special and Inclusive Education, and lives in London.

Kate Bradley had a background in occupational therapy before re-training as a teacher. She has worked in both mainstream and special needs schools, making the lessons fun and engaging for SEN learners. Kate holds a Masters in Special and Inclusive Education, and lives in London.